THE
ISRAELI-PALESTINIAN
CONFLICT

A Beginner's Guide to Objective Understanding
Through a Fact-Based Journey
From Past to Present

Written by
Peter Schwartzman

Table of Contents

SOME NOTABLE QUOTES (*)

"We will not solve the Israeli-Palestinian conflict militarily, nor will they."

Ehud Olmert, former Prime Minister of Israel (2007)

"Palestine and Israel are geographical areas, not nations, nor unique peoples."

Edward Said, Palestinian-American literary theorist and public intellectual (1999)

"It won't be easy. Peace never is. There are powerful interests that are invested in the status quo. And there are people on both sides who have not yet overcome the heavy burdens of mutual mistrust."

Barack Obama, former President of the United States (2013)

"This is a conflict that has lasted for almost a century. With every passing day it becomes more complicated, more difficult to resolve."

King Hussein I of Jordan (1991)

"Let us partition as friends, and not divide as enemies. Israel will be there next to Palestine, and if need be, we shall defend the state of Palestine."

David Ben-Gurion, the first Prime Minister of Israel (1937)

(*) Some quotes might be slightly paraphrased or abridged for clarity, and their interpretation can be subject to context and perspective. The perspectives and views on peace, complexity, and solutions have been various and multifaceted throughout the years, reflecting the ongoing difficulty in navigating this prolonged conflict.

Prelude: An Ancient Land, a Modern Quandary

A Timeless Struggle

In the rolling hills of the Levant, where olive trees have grown for millennia and ancient roads have witnessed countless migrations, the land tells stories that span thousands of years. This terrain, with its haunting beauty and strategic significance, has been the envy of empires and the aspiration of diverse civilizations. The land that is now referred to as Israel and Palestine is not just another parcel on the map; it's a place deeply woven into the fabric of human history.

Ancient civilizations once flourished here. The Canaanites built their cities, the Israelites established their first kingdoms, and the Philistines confronted early Hebrew tribes. King Solomon erected a temple in Jerusalem, which would later be destroyed, rebuilt, and razed again, only to become the foundation for future spiritual centers. Through the centuries, Assyrians, Babylonians, Persians, Greeks, and Romans left their marks, each bringing their own narrative, ambition, and often, conflict.

Fast forward to today's urban scapes, and the historical layers become more palpable. Walk through Jerusalem's Old City, and you traverse through time. Cobblestone streets echo with millennia of history. A modern tramway in the city passes by walls and fortifications that have witnessed countless sieges and conquests. Nearby, Tel Aviv buzzes as a cosmopolitan center with beachfront cafes, towering skyscrapers, and booming tech startups, presenting a stark contrast to the age-old disputes it's nestled within.

But the shadow of the past is never truly gone. Even as bustling markets sell high-tech gadgets and trendy fashion, they also offer antiquities and traditional crafts that speak of an older world. Beneath new constructions, archaeologists often find remnants of ancient civilizations. Every new road, building, or park can become a battleground of historical narratives and claims.

This continuum of conflict isn't just about the physical markers on the ground. It's deeply ingrained in the psyche of the people. Stories passed from grandparents to grandchildren speak of heroism, exile, return, and hope. They talk of Jerusalem's ancient temples, Jaffa's port where Jonah once fled, Bethlehem's starry night, or Hebron's sacred tombs. And in these stories, history isn't a distant concept; it's a living, breathing presence.

For both Palestinians and Israelis, the land represents home, identity, and belonging. Their historical narratives, while distinct, overlap in geography and time. The land has seen Solomon's wisdom and Saladin's valor, the Maccabees' revolt and modern intifadas. And while the earth beneath has absorbed tales of unity, love, and coexistence, it has also, tragically, soaked up much blood and tears.

In the end, the timeless struggle isn't just about who came first or who has the mightier claim. It's about acknowledging the intricate tapestry of histories, emotions, and aspirations that make this small piece of earth immensely significant. It's about understanding that until both sides recognize and respect the other's connection to the land, peace will remain elusive.

Stories from Ground Zero

On a narrow alleyway in Ramallah, a breeze ruffles the embroidered edges of Haneen's hijab. A cup of sage tea in her hand, she gazes at the children playing outside, their laughter echoing in the courtyard. The patterns on the tiles beneath her feet, she recalls, were much like the ones in her ancestral home, surrounded by an expansive olive orchard, the pride of her family.

"I was but a girl," Haneen starts, her eyes distant with memories, "when I would accompany my father to the orchard. The aroma of the olive trees during harvest season, the rustle of leaves, and the joy in my father's eyes as he looked at the yield... it was all magical. Those trees were not just plants; they were symbols of our roots, deeply embedded in the land. They bore witness to weddings, births, feasts, and sorrows."

She recalls the tales her father told her as they rested under an ancient olive tree, stories of their ancestors who had tended to the same trees, of harvest festivals, and of times when neighbors, irrespective of their faith, would come together to celebrate life. "The orchard," she says, "wasn't just a piece of land. It was where our past met our present."

A few hundred kilometers away, in a café in Haifa, Yaron sits with a mixed feeling of pride and anxiety, watching a news report about the Israeli Defense Forces. His daughter, Noa, just turned 18 and has begun her mandatory military service.

"She's always been so spirited," Yaron says, looking at a photo of a younger Noa playing on the beach. "Even as a child, she had this sense of purpose, this belief that she had a role to play for her country." As a father, Yaron had hoped for a different path for her, perhaps studying at a university, traveling, or starting her own venture. But he also understood the deep-seated sense of duty Noa felt.

"Every generation of our family has served," he continues. "My grandfather fought for the state's independence. I was in the unit that guarded our borders. And now, Noa wears her uniform with that same pride." But behind Yaron's pride, there's an unmistakable fear. "I've seen the costs of conflict up close. And as a parent, you wish your children would be spared from it. But this is our reality."

Two stories, two lives, and two different perspectives. Haneen's memories of an idyllic past and the loss of her ancestral land contrast with Yaron's contemporary fears and hopes for his daughter's future. Yet, both tales converge on one point: a deep-rooted connection to the same land and the lengths they'd go to protect their version of home. Their stories reflect the human side of a geopolitical struggle, where personal narratives intertwine with national histories, making the Palestinian-Israeli conflict not just a matter of borders and rights but also of hearts and minds.

The Complex Web of Peace

In the intricate ballet of international diplomacy, few dances have been as intricate, as heartfelt, and at times, as tragic as the efforts to secure peace between Israel and Palestine. This journey, riddled with highs and lows, moments of hope and despair, encapsulates the challenges of reconciling deeply rooted historical narratives, divergent aspirations, and geopolitical realities.

1. The Early Gestures

In the aftermath of the 1967 Six-Day War, the UN Security Council passed Resolution 242, calling for Israel's withdrawal from territories occupied in the war and the recognition of every state's right to live in peace. This laid the groundwork for future negotiations, emphasizing the "land for peace" principle. Yet, peace remained distant, as mistrust ran deep and the tangible steps toward compromise were hard to discern.

2. Camp David Accords (1978)

Perhaps the first significant breakthrough came in the form of the Camp David Accords under the stewardship of US

President Jimmy Carter. Israeli Prime Minister Menachem Begin and Egyptian President Anwar Sadat, in a testament to their leadership and vision, agreed upon a framework that would lead to the historic Egypt-Israel Peace Treaty in 1979. While this was a bilateral achievement, it set a precedent for Arab-Israeli peace and showed that diplomacy, however challenging, was possible.

3. The Oslo Accords (1990s)

The 1990s brought a fresh wave of optimism. The secret negotiations in Norway led to the 1993 Oslo Accords, signed with a historic handshake between Yitzhak Rabin and Yasser Arafat on the White House lawn. For the first time, Palestinians gained self-rule in parts of the West Bank and Gaza. However, the euphoria was short-lived. The assassination of Rabin, escalating violence, and political shifts on both sides meant that the envisioned two-state solution was still out of reach.

4. The 2000 Camp David Summit

Hopes were rekindled when US President Bill Clinton mediated talks between Israeli Prime Minister Ehud Barak and Palestinian leader Yasser Arafat. However, the gaps, especially on issues like the status of Jerusalem and Palestinian refugees, proved too wide. The summit's failure was followed by the outbreak of the Second Intifada, signaling another low point in peace efforts.

5. The Arab Peace Initiative (2002)

Introduced by then-Crown Prince Abdullah of Saudi Arabia, the Arab Peace Initiative offered full normalization of relations between the Arab world and Israel, in exchange for Israel's complete withdrawal from occupied territories, including East Jerusalem, and a "just resolution" for Palestinian refugees. While this initiative reoriented the regional dialogue, direct Israeli-Palestinian negotiations continued to face roadblocks.

6. The Annapolis Conference (2007) and After

Under the auspices of US President George W. Bush, Israeli and Palestinian leaders once again committed to working towards a two-state solution. But concrete progress remained elusive due to changing political landscapes, continued settlements, and divisions within the Palestinian leadership.

So, why has peace remained so elusive? The reasons are manifold:

- **Divergent Narratives**: Both sides have deeply rooted historical narratives and spiritual connections to the land, leading to non-negotiable demands and a lack of mutual recognition.
- **Geopolitical Realities**: Regional powers, each with their own agendas, often influenced the trajectory of peace talks.
- **Internal Divisions**: Both Israelis and Palestinians have faced internal political fragmentation, making consensus-building challenging.
- **Trust Deficit**: Repeated cycles of violence, provocations, and perceived betrayals have eroded trust, making compromises even more difficult.

The journey towards peace has been a complex web of diplomacy, interspersed with moments of hope and despair. Yet, the aspiration for a peaceful coexistence remains, rooted in the belief that the shared history of the land can one day translate into a shared future.

Introduction

Purpose of the Book

In the vast expanse of human history, there are conflicts that have shaped civilizations, stories that have molded nations, and narratives so profound that they've changed the course of the world. The Israeli-Palestinian issue is one such narrative. But why delve into this particular story now? And why seek another addition to the already extensive literature on the topic? The purpose of this book is manifold:

- **Bridging Knowledge Gaps**: While the Israeli-Palestinian conflict often makes headlines, the nuances, histories, and human stories behind the news articles are frequently lost. This book aims to offer readers an in-depth look, moving beyond surface-level information.
- **Balanced Insight**: In an age where information is often polarized, presenting a balanced perspective is crucial. This book endeavors to portray the narratives of both sides, allowing readers to draw their own informed conclusions.
- **Humanizing the Conflict**: Often, geopolitical disputes are seen in abstract terms—maps, treaties, and high-level summits. By weaving in personal stories and anecdotes, this book hopes to bring to the forefront the lives, dreams, and aspirations of the people who live this conflict every day.
- **Contextualizing the Role of the US**: The United States, given its geopolitical influence and historical involvement, plays a unique role in the Israeli-Palestinian dynamics. For American readers, understanding this role is not just about foreign policy

but also about introspecting on the larger ideals the country stands for.

- **Inspiring Engagement**: The ultimate goal is not just to inform but to inspire. An informed reader becomes a conscious global citizen, capable of engaging in constructive conversations, advocating for peace, and supporting initiatives that bring communities closer.
- **Setting a Foundation for the Future**: The youth of today will inherit the world of tomorrow. By equipping them with knowledge, empathy, and a deeper understanding, we can hope for a generation that champions dialogue over discord, collaboration over conflict.

In penning this book, the intention is not to provide definitive solutions or to claim the moral high ground. It is, quite simply, to shed light, to foster understanding, and to remind us all that at the heart of every geopolitical issue are human beings, with their stories, hopes, and dreams. And in understanding these stories, perhaps, lies the key to unlocking a more peaceful future.

Overview of the Palestinian-Israeli Conflict

The Palestinian-Israeli conflict, often cited in news headlines and debated in international forums, is one of the world's longest-standing and most contentious geopolitical disputes. At its core, it revolves around competing nationalisms and the struggle for a homeland on a piece of land in the Eastern Mediterranean, roughly the size of New Jersey.

This land, historically known for its cultural and religious significance, is sacred to Jews, Muslims, and Christians. Its cities, like Jerusalem, Bethlehem, and Hebron, hold deep religious and historical importance. The contestation for control and ownership of this region, and the narratives surrounding it, lie at the heart of the Palestinian-Israeli issue.

From the Palestinian perspective, the story is one of displacement, loss, and a quest for statehood. Starting with the early 20th century, waves of Jewish immigrants arrived in Palestine, then under British colonial rule. Over time, tensions escalated between the Arab majority and the growing Jewish community. The UN's decision in 1947 to partition the land into an Arab and a Jewish state was seen by Palestinians as an affront to their majority status in the territory. The subsequent establishment of the State of Israel in 1948 led to a war and the displacement of hundreds of thousands of Palestinians from their homes, an event they commemorate as the Nakba, or "catastrophe."

For Israelis, the narrative is about the reestablishment of a Jewish homeland after millennia of exile and persecution. The traumas of history, particularly the Holocaust, cemented the desire for a safe haven for the Jewish people. The establishment of Israel was seen as the realization of this aspiration. In this context, the wars and conflicts that followed are often viewed as existential battles for the survival of the Jewish state.

Complicating the matter further are the territories Israel occupied after the 1967 Six-Day War: the West Bank, Gaza Strip, and East Jerusalem. These areas are home to millions of Palestinians and have been the sites of Israeli settlements, which are deemed illegal under international law. The presence of settlements, the security measures employed by Israel, and the administration of these territories have been focal points of tension and conflict.

The intricate web of issues — the right of return for Palestinian refugees, the status of Jerusalem (a city sacred to both), the borders of a potential Palestinian state, the presence of Israeli settlements, and concerns about security and recognition — make the Palestinian-Israeli conflict incredibly challenging to resolve. Each side has deep-seated fears, historical traumas, and genuine aspirations that often seem incompatible with the other's vision for the future.

Additionally, internal divisions within both the Israeli and Palestinian communities and the influence of regional and global powers further muddy the waters. The diversity of voices, from hardline to conciliatory, affects the pace and direction of peace talks.

Understanding the Palestinian-Israeli issue is not just about knowing the sequence of events or the details of failed peace deals. It's about recognizing the depth of emotion, identity, and history that both Palestinians and Israelis attach to the land they both call home. It's about understanding why compromises that seem logical on paper are so hard to enact on the ground.

As we delve deeper into this topic, it becomes evident that understanding the present complexities of the Palestinian-Israeli conflict is impossible without a grasp of its history. The following chapters will provide a historical backdrop, tracing the roots of this issue and exploring the events that have shaped the narratives of both communities. By studying the past, we aim to provide a clearer lens to view the present and envision a future where coexistence might be possible.

Part I: Historical Background

Chapter 1: Ancient Roots

Ancient Canaan and Early Inhabitants

Long before the term "Middle East" was coined, and millennia before the headlines of today, the land now often referred to as Israel-Palestine was known as Canaan. Nestled at the crossroads of continents, this land has always been more than just a plot of earth—it's been a tapestry of cultures, stories, and civilizations.

Imagine a time when the vast Mediterranean stretched out, a shimmering blue, and the fertile crescent arched across the region. Canaan was a gem in the center, kissed by sun and sea, cradled by ancient civilizations. Its position made it both blessed and cursed; blessed because of its bountiful resources and cursed because empires often eyed it for conquest.

The earliest inhabitants of Canaan were a melting pot of peoples, each bringing with them a blend of traditions, gods, and ways of life. They established city-states, like Jericho, one of the world's oldest inhabited cities. These Canaanites were not just passive residents; they were traders, artisans, and innovators. Their influence spread through trade networks, connecting them to the wider ancient world from Egypt to Mesopotamia.

Over time, various groups migrated or invaded this land. Among them were the Hebrews, who, according to biblical accounts, arrived in Canaan after a sojourn in Egypt. Their story, marked by covenant, exile, and return, laid the spiritual foundation for what would later become Judaism. The land bore witness to their tales, from the patriarch Abraham's journey to the kingdom of David and Solomon.

But Canaan was not just the stage for biblical narratives. The Pharaohs of Egypt, drawn by its allure, often ventured into Canaan, leaving behind relics and inscriptions. The land also felt the march of Assyrian boots and the sweep of the Babylonian empire. Each empire that touched Canaan left behind a layer, adding to its rich mosaic.

In essence, Canaan was a meeting ground—a place where histories intertwined, where cultures melded, and where ancient stories were carved into the very stones. This vibrant past, echoing with tales of faith, trade, and transformation, set the stage for the later events that would define the region.

As we journey forward from ancient Canaan, it's crucial to remember this foundational era. The land's legacy is not just a backdrop to today's conflict but a testament to a time when diverse peoples coexisted, and a reminder of the deep roots that many have to this storied landscape.

Jewish Kingdoms and Roman Rule

Transitioning from the tales of ancient Canaan, the narrative of the land took a pivotal turn with the rise of the Jewish kingdoms and the shadow of Roman dominion.

The story of the Israelites, having settled in Canaan, began to transform the region's fabric. Under leaders like King David, the Israelites united the Twelve Tribes and established the Kingdom of Israel. David's son, Solomon, further amplified this legacy, constructing the First Temple in Jerusalem, a monumental edifice that not only served as a religious hub but also symbolized the unity and identity of the Jewish people. Jerusalem emerged as more than just a capital; it was the heart of a spiritual and cultural renaissance.

However, like many tales of rise, there were periods of decline. The unified kingdom eventually split into two—Israel in the north and Judah in the south. These separate entities had their destinies intertwined with larger empires, from the Assyrians to the Babylonians. The latter's conquest of Judah led to the destruction of Solomon's Temple and the onset of the Babylonian Exile, a poignant chapter in Jewish history.

But the land, resilient as ever, witnessed a return. The Persians, having toppled the Babylonians, permitted the Jews to return and rebuild. The Second Temple arose, symbolizing rebirth and renewal.

Yet, as the pages of history turned, a new actor entered the scene: the Romans. Initially, their dominion was indirect, supporting local rulers like Herod the Great, known for his grand architectural feats, including the expansion of the Second Temple. But Roman patience with regional autonomy thinned over time, leading to direct rule and the imposition of Roman culture and governance.

The Jews, cherishing their distinct identity and traditions, often found themselves at odds with the Roman overlords. Rebellions flared, the most significant being the Great Jewish Revolt in 66 CE. The aftermath was cataclysmic—the Second Temple, that enduring symbol of Jewish identity, was razed in 70 CE by the Roman legions.

The land, however, was far from silent. Jerusalem, though scarred, remained a beacon. Jewish communities persisted, even as Roman rule morphed into Byzantine control.

This era, marked by grand temples, fervent kings, and the indomitable will of a people, serves as a reminder of the land's eternal dance between cultural assertion and external influence. As we delve deeper into history, these layers, of Jewish kingdoms and Roman rule, shape the evolving tapestry of the region.

Early Christian and Byzantine Periods

As the Roman Empire stretched across continents, a new faith took root within its borders: Christianity. Born in the heart of the land we've journeyed through, this faith transformed not only the spiritual landscape but also the political and cultural realms.

Picture a humble carpenter's son, Jesus of Nazareth, traveling the hills and valleys, preaching a message of love, sacrifice, and redemption. His teachings, initially modest in reach, resonated deeply and spread like wildfire. By the time of his crucifixion in Jerusalem, Jesus had garnered a following, and within a few decades, this nascent faith began to challenge the established religious order.

A turning point arrived with the conversion of Saul, a persecutor of Christians, on the road to Damascus. Reborn as Paul, his missionary journeys and letters breathed life into Christian communities across the Roman world.

Now, here's a twist one might not expect: the Roman Empire, which once saw Christianity as a threat, embraced it. In the early 4th century, Emperor Constantine the Great experienced a dramatic conversion. Legend has it that before a crucial battle, Constantine saw a cross in the sky with the inscription "In this sign, you will conquer." He emerged victorious and attributed his success to the Christian God. With the Edict of Milan in 313 CE, he granted religious tolerance to Christians, laying the groundwork for Christianity's ascendance as the state religion.

Under Constantine's reign, the landscape of our storied land underwent a metamorphosis. The city of Jerusalem, scarred by prior revolts, was revitalized. The Church of the Holy Sepulchre, believed to be the site of Jesus' crucifixion and resurrection, was erected, drawing pilgrims from distant lands.

The transition from Roman to Byzantine rule heralded an era where Christian art, architecture, and scholarship flourished. Byzantine emperors, seeing themselves as God's representatives on earth, adorned the land with churches, monasteries, and mosaics.

Yet, it wasn't all a golden age. Internal theological disputes created rifts within the Christian community. Debates over the nature of Christ, for instance, led to councils and sometimes exiles and persecutions.

As the Byzantine period unfolded, the land, with Jerusalem at its heart, became a mosaic of Christian sects, each with its own interpretation of faith, yet all bound by the shared history of a carpenter who once walked its streets.

The echoes of this era, with its blend of faith, art, and empire, continue to reverberate. As we journey forward, it's essential to recognize the profound impact of the early Christian and Byzantine periods, an era when the spiritual met the imperial, shaping the destiny of the land and its people.

Chapter 2: Arab and Ottoman Rule

Early Islamic Conquests

In the shifting sands of history, as the Byzantine Empire basked in its Christian glory, a new wind blew from the deserts of Arabia, carrying with it a fresh revelation and a faith destined to reshape the world: Islam.

It all began with Muhammad, a merchant from Mecca, who in the early 7th century, retreated to a cave for contemplation. There, he reported receiving divine messages from the angel Gabriel. These revelations, meticulously recorded, formed the Qur'an, the holy scripture of Islam.

Muhammad's teachings of monotheism, social justice, and community spread rapidly across the Arabian Peninsula, uniting tribes and birthing a new religious and political entity.

Now, an intriguing tale often recounted is of the Prophet's night journey. Legend has it that one evening, Muhammad was miraculously transported from Mecca to Jerusalem, where he ascended to heaven and communed with past prophets. This event, though brief, firmly anchored Jerusalem's significance in Islamic tradition.

By the mid-7th century, bolstered by their faith and led by the Rashidun Caliphs, Muslim armies began their series of expeditions beyond Arabia. The Byzantine and Sassanian empires, grand as they were, had been weakened by years of conflict. This, coupled with the zeal of the Muslim warriors and the allure of the new faith, allowed for swift Islamic conquests.

Palestine, with its rich religious tapestry, came under Muslim rule after the Battle of Yarmouk in 636 CE. The transition, by many historical accounts, was relatively smooth, with agreements ensuring safety and religious freedom for the Christian majority. Jerusalem, the city of prophets, opened its gates to the Caliph Umar, who famously declined to pray in the Church of the Holy Sepulchre, not wanting to set a precedent that might endanger its Christian character.

Under Muslim stewardship, the city experienced a renaissance. The crowning jewel was the construction of the Dome of the Rock on the Temple Mount in the late 7th century. With its golden dome shimmering under the Middle Eastern sun, it stood as a testament to Islam's reverence for the city.

The early Islamic period wasn't just about conquests and

architectural feats. It was an era of coexistence, scholarship, and cultural fusion. Christian, Jewish, and Muslim scholars engaged in debates, translated works, and embarked on intellectual quests that enriched the world.

As we continue our journey, it's essential to reflect on this epoch when a new faith arose, not as an isolating force, but one that wove itself seamlessly into the historical and cultural fabric of our ever-evolving land.

Crusades and Christian Rule

The timeline of our storied land has witnessed empires rise and fall, each leaving an indelible mark. As the 11th century dawned, distant murmurs from Europe hinted at another monumental shift: the Crusades, a series of military expeditions aimed at recapturing the Holy Land from its Muslim rulers.

The call was initiated by Pope Urban II in 1095. With impassioned speeches, he rallied the Christian kingdoms of Europe to embark on a holy mission. His words painted vivid images of Christian brethren suffering in the East and the need to liberate the sacred city of Jerusalem. The response was immense; knights, nobles, and peasants alike took up the cross, driven by a mix of piety, adventure, and the allure of potential riches.

In 1099, after a grueling campaign, the First Crusaders breached Jerusalem's walls. Anecdotes from that time paint a harrowing picture. One such account recalls a Crusader, Raymond of Aguilers, expressing awe and horror, saying, "In the Temple and porch of Solomon, men rode in blood up to their knees and bridle reins."

The subsequent establishment of the Latin Kingdom of

Jerusalem marked a new chapter. For nearly two centuries, various Crusader states dotted the region, fortifying their rule with castles and forging alliances. But their dominion was not monolithic; it was punctuated by battles, treaties, and even periods of peaceful coexistence with their Muslim and Jewish subjects.

One intriguing episode during this era was the relationship between Sultan Salah ad-Din (Saladin) and Richard the Lionheart. Despite being adversaries, they shared mutual respect. Legends speak of Saladin sending his personal physician to treat Richard when he fell ill and the two leaders exchanging gifts and courtesies.

However, the Crusader presence wasn't destined to last. Muslim forces, under leaders like Saladin, rallied, recapturing vast territories. By 1291, with the fall of Acre, the Crusader chapter in the Holy Land drew to a close.

In retrospect, the Crusades were more than just battles and sieges. They were a cultural and religious crossroads, where East met West, bringing about trade, translation efforts, and even architectural influences that shaped Gothic Europe.

Yet, the scars of the Crusades lingered. The memory of these fervent campaigns, both their achievements and atrocities, serves as a poignant reminder of the complexities of merging faith with empire and the eternal dance of conflict and coexistence that defines our land.

Ottoman Period

From the vast Anatolian plains arose an empire that would come to define the fate of our land for centuries: the Ottoman Empire. Founded in the 13th century, by the time the 16th century rolled around, the Ottomans, under the leadership of Sultan Selim I, set their sights on the Middle East.

By 1517, the Ottomans had claimed the heart of the Arab world, including Egypt and, significantly, Palestine. This territorial conquest, while primarily political and military in nature, was also symbolic. With Jerusalem under its belt, the Ottoman Empire now controlled all three major Abrahamic holy cities: Mecca, Medina, and Jerusalem.

Under Ottoman rule, the land experienced an era of relative stability and development. Infrastructure projects, such as roads and water systems, were undertaken, and cities like Jerusalem, Jaffa, and Haifa experienced growth. Religious communities—Muslims, Christians, and Jews—generally coexisted under the Ottoman policy of millets, which granted religious minorities a degree of autonomy.

An intriguing vignette from this era revolves around the city's walls. In the early 16th century, Sultan Suleiman the Magnificent, upon hearing a dream that hinted at the city's vulnerability, ordered the construction of the imposing walls around Jerusalem's Old City. Those very walls, with their ornate gates and fortifications, stand resilient to this day, a testament to Suleiman's vision.

Yet, the Ottoman period wasn't without challenges. As the empire grew, so did administrative difficulties. By the 19th century, with European powers vying for influence and internal issues festering, the empire's grip began to wane. Innovations like the construction of the Hejaz Railway, aiming to solidify control, were counteracted by the empire's decentralization and external pressures.

Adding to the complexities, the late 19th and early 20th centuries witnessed the stirrings of Zionist aspirations. Jewish immigrants, motivated by both spiritual and nationalist impulses, began settling in Palestine, often purchasing land and establishing communities. This immigration, while initially limited, set the stage for dynamics that would soon envelop the region.

As the sun set on World War I, so too did it mark the twilight of the Ottoman Empire. Palestine, like many other Ottoman territories, was on the cusp of a new chapter, one filled with promise, challenges, and profound transformations.

Reflecting on the Ottoman period, it emerges not just as an epoch of dominion but also as a crucible of cultures, where traditions intermingled, and the seeds of future narratives were sown.

Chapter 3: Zionism and Arab Nationalism

Emergence of Zionism

As the 19th century unfolded in Europe, waves of nationalism swept across nations, awakening collective identities and dreams of statehood. Amid this fervor, a movement arose within the Jewish diaspora, rooted in millennia of spiritual yearning and further catalyzed by contemporary challenges: Zionism.

Zionism's essence was the aspiration for a national homeland for the Jewish people in Palestine, the biblical land of Zion. While the yearning for a return to Zion had been embedded in Jewish prayers for centuries, the modern Zionist movement was also a response to rising anti-Semitism, particularly in Eastern Europe and Russia.

The spark of this modern drive can be traced to Theodor Herzl, a Viennese journalist. An anecdote from Herzl's life captures the turning point. After covering the Dreyfus Affair in 1894, where a Jewish French army captain was wrongfully accused of treason amid a backdrop of anti-Semitic fervor,

Herzl penned "The Jewish State." This treatise laid out the vision for a sovereign Jewish state, not necessarily in Palestine but anywhere that offered refuge from persecution.

The movement quickly gained momentum. In 1897, Herzl convened the First Zionist Congress in Basel, Switzerland, bringing together diverse Jewish factions under the banner of Zionism. By this time, the focus had solidified on Palestine as the desired homeland.

Parallel to the ideological development, practical steps were taken. Early Zionist pioneers, known as the "First Aliyah," began arriving in Ottoman-controlled Palestine in the late 19th century. These settlers, motivated by both spiritual and nationalist impulses, bought lands, established farms, and founded new communities.

Yet, the Zionist movement was far from monolithic. Visions for the future state varied. Some imagined a socialist utopia, others a haven preserving traditional Jewish culture, and still, others focused on forging a new, uniquely Israeli identity.

But as the Jewish presence in Palestine grew, so did tensions. The indigenous Arab population, witnessing the influx and fearing for their future in the land, expressed increasing unease. This friction, initially limited, was an omen of more significant conflicts in the decades to come.

In concluding our foray into the emergence of Zionism, we glimpse a tapestry of hope, resilience, and challenge. A movement birthed from centuries of yearning and the urgencies of its time, Zionism would play a pivotal role in shaping the destinies of both the Jewish people and the broader Middle Eastern landscape.

Early Jewish Settlements

With the dawn of Zionism came the material realization of its dreams. As ideas transformed into action, Jewish pioneers, filled with passion and purpose, began making their way to Palestine's shores, sowing the seeds of early Jewish settlements.

The late 19th and early 20th centuries marked the waves of these migrations, known as 'Aliyahs.' The First Aliyah, between 1882 and 1903, saw primarily Eastern European Jews arrive. These pioneers, often fleeing pogroms and persecution, were driven by a blend of religious aspiration and the desire for a better life in their ancestral homeland.

Among the settlements of this period was Rishon LeZion. Founded in 1882, its name meaning "First to Zion," it truly embodied the spirit of these times. Here, settlers grappled with malarial swamps and harsh conditions. But their persistence bore fruit, both metaphorically and literally, as they transformed challenging terrains into flourishing vineyards, signaling a promising start.

The Second Aliyah, spanning 1904 to 1914, differed in character. Many of these immigrants were young idealists, inspired by socialist ideals. They not only aimed to establish Jewish homes but also aspired to reshape society. They introduced the kibbutz – collective communities that emphasized shared resources, egalitarian principles, and a deep bond with the land.

An intriguing episode from this period involves a young woman named Manya Shochat. Dubbed the "mother of the kibbutz," Manya passionately believed in collective living. Legend has it that, during a heated debate on communal life, she dramatically placed a pot in the room's center, declaring it communal property, encapsulating the kibbutz spirit in one symbolic gesture.

Yet, these early settlements were not without contention. While the Jewish pioneers saw themselves reclaiming a historic homeland, the native Arab populace viewed the increasing land purchases and Jewish immigration with growing concern. The land, once shared by multiple communities, was becoming a stage for competing national narratives.

As we reflect on the early Jewish settlements, we witness a blend of dreams actualized and challenges encountered. These communities, forged in determination and idealism, laid foundational stones for the future State of Israel. But in their shadows were also the nascent complexities and tensions that would define the region in the century to come.

Arab Nationalist Movements

Parallel to the burgeoning Zionist aspirations in Palestine was the rise of Arab nationalism across the Middle East. As the 20th century dawned, many Arabs, united by linguistic, cultural, and historical ties, yearned to shake off the yoke of Ottoman rule and later, European imperial interests, dreaming of autonomy, unity, and sovereignty.

This nationalist fervor germinated during the late Ottoman period. The idea of 'Arabism' or 'Arab unity' began taking root, especially among intellectuals, military officers, and urban elites. They envisioned a united Arab state stretching from the Arabian Peninsula to the Levant.

One iconic figure from this period was Sharif Hussein of Mecca. Hoping to establish an independent Arab kingdom, he allied with the British during World War I and led the Arab Revolt against the Ottomans in 1916. The revolt, though militarily limited, was symbolically significant, with the

Hashemite forces taking control of key territories, including Damascus.

A fascinating anecdote from this period concerns Lawrence of Arabia, a British officer and diplomat. Lawrence formed close ties with Arab leaders, including Faisal, Sharif Hussein's son. Their collaboration, marred by mutual suspicion and British imperial interests, was poignantly captured in the scene where Lawrence and Faisal lit a railway track on fire, symbolizing the disruption of Ottoman control.

However, post-WWI, the high hopes of Arab nationalism faced setbacks. The 1916 Sykes-Picot Agreement between Britain and France carved up the Middle East, disregarding Arab aspirations. Consequently, various Arab territories fell under British and French mandates, including Palestine, where the Balfour Declaration had also promised a "national home for the Jewish people," further complicating the landscape.

In Palestine, the increasing Jewish immigration and land acquisitions fueled Arab concerns. The 1920s and 1930s saw rising tensions, leading to widespread protests and revolts. The Arab Higher Committee, under Haj Amin al-Husseini, emerged as a notable force, advocating for Arab rights and opposing Zionist objectives.

The journey of Arab nationalism, from the dreams of unity to the realities of fragmentation, offers a poignant tale of a region's aspirations, external interventions, and the multifaceted challenges of nation-building. As with the Jewish narrative, the Arab quest for self-determination and identity remains integral to understanding the complex tapestry of the Middle Eastern saga.

Chapter 4: British Mandate Era

Balfour Declaration and its Implications

In the annals of Middle Eastern history, few documents have wielded as much influence as the Balfour Declaration. A mere 67 words, written during the tumult of World War I, this British statement would ripple across the decades, shaping destinies and narratives in the land of Palestine.

Penned on November 2, 1917, by British Foreign Secretary Arthur James Balfour to Lord Walter Rothschild, a leader in the British Jewish community, the declaration asserted: "His Majesty's government view with favour the establishment in Palestine of a national home for the Jewish people... it being clearly understood that nothing shall be done which may prejudice the civil and religious rights of existing non-Jewish communities in Palestine..."

At its heart, the Balfour Declaration was a product of British wartime strategy, a bid to secure Jewish support against the Central Powers. However, for Zionists, it was a monumental victory, the first formal recognition by a major power of Jewish national aspirations in Palestine.

Yet, the ambiguity of the declaration's wording would prove fateful. What did a "national home" mean? How would the rights of the "non-Jewish communities" – the majority Arab population – be safeguarded?

An illuminating anecdote underscores the complexities of the period. Chaim Weizmann, a leading Zionist figure, once met with Balfour and remarked on the historic bond of the Jewish people to Palestine. Balfour, in his characteristic wit, quipped, "It is curious. The Jews I meet are quite different." To which Weizmann retorted, "Mr. Balfour, you meet the wrong kind of Jews."

However, for the Arab inhabitants, the Balfour Declaration was perceived as a betrayal, particularly after the promises made to Sharif Hussein of Mecca about Arab independence. As the 1920s unfolded, tensions escalated. Arab leaders felt sidelined, their aspirations overshadowed by the promises made to the Zionists.

The implications of the Balfour Declaration were vast. It set Britain on a path of mandate governance in Palestine, under the auspices of the League of Nations. It also intensified Jewish immigration, further exacerbating Arab-Jewish relations.

In essence, the Balfour Declaration, brief as it was, became a cornerstone in the edifice of the Palestinian-Israeli conflict. It symbolized hope for some, disillusionment for others, and the intricate challenge of reconciling competing national dreams on a shared land.

Arab Revolts and Jewish Resistance

The period between the World Wars in Palestine was marked by increasing tensions, as the promises and policies of external powers began to bear fruit on the ground. As Jewish immigration surged, facilitated by the Balfour Declaration, the indigenous Arab population grew restive, feeling the pressure of demographic shifts and land acquisitions.

The peak of Arab discontent was the Great Arab Revolt of 1936-1939. Triggered by socio-political frustrations and economic hardships, this uprising saw strikes, boycotts, and armed confrontations against both British mandate authorities and Jewish settlements. The British responded with a heavy hand, deploying large military contingents and employing collective punishments. The revolt eventually led to the Peel Commission of 1937, which recommended the partition of Palestine, an idea met with fierce opposition from Arab leaders.

Parallel to Arab movements, Jewish defense and resistance groups began to take shape. The Haganah, initially a loose organization to defend Jewish communities, evolved into a more formidable force. More radical offshoots emerged, like the Irgun and the Stern Gang (Lehi), which targeted British and Arab adversaries alike.

A particularly poignant anecdote from this era involves Avshalom Feinberg, an early Jewish spy for the British against the Ottomans. Legend has it that, after being killed by Bedouins, a palm tree mysteriously sprouted from his grave, leading his comrades to discover his resting place years later. To this day, Feinberg's memory intertwines with the Palmach, an elite Haganah strike force, illustrating the intimate connection between the land and its narratives.

The tug-of-war for Palestine intensified with both sides using varying degrees of force and diplomacy. It became clear that British policies, often conflicting and reactionary, were exacerbating an already volatile situation. By the end of World War II, as the horrors of the Holocaust came to light, the urgency for a Jewish homeland gained international momentum, setting the stage for a new chapter in this millennia-old land: the birth of the state of Israel and the subsequent struggles of the Palestinian people.

The UN Partition Plan and the End of the Mandate

The years following World War II bore witness to monumental changes on the global stage, and the territory of Palestine was no exception. With the Holocaust's horrors fresh in the world's consciousness, the plight of Jewish refugees and the call for a Jewish homeland became paramount in international discourse.

By 1947, Britain, wearied from war and unable to reconcile the competing nationalisms of Jews and Arabs, decided to pass the Palestine problem to the fledgling United Nations. The UN, taking the mantle, formed a special committee (UNSCOP) to investigate and recommend a solution. After months of deliberation, the committee proposed the partition of Palestine into separate Jewish and Arab states, with Jerusalem as an internationalized city.

On November 29, 1947, the UN General Assembly voted on Resolution 181, endorsing the partition plan. The result was clear: 33 in favor, 13 against, with 10 abstentions. Jubilation erupted in Jewish communities. However, for the Arab populace and neighboring Arab states, this decision was a bitter pill, one they refused to swallow. They viewed the partition as an imposition, a violation of the rights of the majority Arab population in Palestine.

An evocative anecdote from that period centers on Golda Meir, who would later become Israel's Prime Minister. On hearing the UN's decision, she remarked, "For two thousand years, we waited for our homeland. We are willing to wait another half hour." A testament to the depth of longing for a nation, but also a hint at the impending challenges post-declaration.

The months following the UN decision were tumultuous. Violence between Jewish and Arab communities escalated. As the British Mandate's end neared, on May 14, 1948, David Ben-Gurion declared the establishment of the State of Israel. Immediately, neighboring Arab countries intervened, setting off the 1948 Arab-Israeli war.

The UN's partition plan, envisioned as a fair solution, ended up setting the stage for decades of conflict. The end of the British Mandate did not mark an end to strife in Palestine; rather, it was the beginning of a new, even more complex chapter.

Chapter 5: Statehood and Wars

Creation of Israel and the 1948 War

The proclamation of the State of Israel on May 14, 1948, was a watershed moment in Middle Eastern history. For Jews around the world, it marked the culmination of millennia of dreams and decades of modern political activism. However, for the Palestinian Arabs and neighboring countries, it signaled a challenge to their territorial and nationalistic aspirations.

Hours after Israel's declaration, a coalition of Arab states, including Egypt, Syria, Jordan, Lebanon, and Iraq, launched a military intervention with the aim of thwarting the newly declared state. What ensued is commonly referred to as the 1948 Arab-Israeli war or by Palestinians as Nakba (meaning 'catastrophe').

The conflict was fierce and fraught with both tactical battles and broader symbolic struggles. By its end in 1949, Israel had not only survived but also expanded its territory beyond the original UN partition proposal. Armistice lines, commonly known as the Green Line, were drawn, marking tentative borders but not a lasting peace.

Yet, beyond the strategic gains and losses, the human cost was immense. An estimated 700,000 Palestinians fled or were expelled from their homes, leading to a refugee crisis that resonates to this day. Jewish communities in the Arab world also faced backlash, resulting in mass migrations to Israel.

A touching anecdote from this era is the story of a Jewish fighter who, upon entering the Old City of Jerusalem, pressed a note into the Western Wall that read: "May peace descend upon the whole house of Israel." The weight of history, religion, and newfound sovereignty combined in that moment, reflecting the complex tapestry of emotions experienced by many during that time.

The 1948 war left an indelible mark on the region. It solidified Israel's place on the map but sowed seeds of resentment, displacement, and unresolved political issues. A nascent nation celebrated its birth, even as neighboring states and displaced Palestinians grappled with a new reality, setting the stage for decades of contention.

1956 Suez Crisis

Less than a decade after the tumultuous events of 1948, the Middle East was once again thrust into the spotlight with the Suez Crisis of 1956. At its core, this conflict was about control, nationalism, and the lingering shadows of colonial influence.

Egyptian President Gamal Abdel Nasser, a charismatic figure who championed Arab nationalism, nationalized the Suez Canal in July 1956. This vital waterway, linking the Mediterranean to the Red Sea, was a symbol of Western imperialism, having been controlled by British and French interests.

Nasser's move was not merely symbolic; it threatened Western strategic and economic interests. In response, a secret agreement was hatched between Britain, France, and

Israel. Israel would invade the Sinai Peninsula, giving Britain and France a pretext to intervene ostensibly to separate the warring parties, but in reality to regain control of the canal.

In late October, the plan was set into motion. Israeli forces quickly advanced, capturing much of Sinai. Then, British and French paratroopers were dropped over the Canal Zone. However, the intervention faced staunch opposition, not only from Egypt but also from a global community wary of colonial undertones. The United States and the Soviet Union, usually on opposing sides during the Cold War, both condemned the tripartite invasion.

An intriguing anecdote from this episode involves U.S. President Dwight D. Eisenhower. When informed of the invasion, he reportedly exclaimed, "I've just never seen great powers make such a complete mess and botch of things." His frustration underscored the geopolitical implications of the crisis, particularly during the Cold War era.

Under immense international pressure, including financial threats from the U.S., the invading forces withdrew by March 1957. While Nasser did not emerge militarily victorious, politically, he was strengthened, hailed as the champion who stood up to Western imperialism.

The Suez Crisis, though brief, reshaped geopolitics. It signaled the decline of British and French colonial influence in the region and highlighted the growing importance of the U.S. and the Soviet Union in Middle Eastern affairs. The events of 1956 further complicated the Arab-Israeli conflict, sowing seeds for future confrontations.

1967 Six-Day War and its Aftermath

By the mid-1960s, tensions in the Middle East had escalated to a precipice. Mutual distrust and sporadic skirmishes between Israel and its Arab neighbors had created a powder keg awaiting a spark. That spark came in 1967, leading to a swift and momentous conflict known as the Six-Day War.

In the weeks leading up to the war, Egyptian forces, responding to false reports of Israeli troop concentrations, began amassing in the Sinai Peninsula. Additionally, Egypt imposed a naval blockade on the Straits of Tiran, a critical waterway for Israel. These actions, coupled with bellicose rhetoric and alliances between Egypt, Syria, and Jordan, convinced Israel that a coordinated Arab attack was imminent.

On June 5, Israel launched a pre-emptive airstrike, decimating the air forces of Egypt and Syria. With air superiority achieved, Israeli ground forces moved rapidly, capturing the Sinai from Egypt, the Golan Heights from Syria, and the West Bank and East Jerusalem from Jordan.

In just six days, the map of the Middle East was redrawn. Israel had more than doubled its size, but more importantly, it had changed the strategic balance of the region.

An anecdote that captures the emotional weight of the war concerns the reunification of Jerusalem. Israeli paratroopers, upon reaching the Western Wall, a holy Jewish site, were moved to tears. Their commander, Mordechai "Motta" Gur, emotionally broadcasted, "The Temple Mount is in our hands!" That message resonated deeply with Jews worldwide, encapsulating centuries of yearning for Jerusalem.

However, the aftermath of the war was less clear-cut. Israel's territorial gains brought with it a large Palestinian population, presenting both a demographic challenge and a political conundrum. While Israel offered to exchange land for peace, the Arab League, meeting in Khartoum, issued their infamous "Three No's": No peace with Israel, no recognition of Israel, no negotiations with Israel.

The 1967 war, while a military masterclass, laid the groundwork for decades of occupation, settlement expansion, and persistent regional animosity. The debate over the territories captured during those six days continues to be at the heart of the Israeli-Palestinian conflict.

1973 Yom Kippur War

Just six years after the swift and stunning victory of the Six-Day War, Israel found itself taken by surprise in a conflict that would shake its confidence and redefine Middle Eastern geopolitics: the Yom Kippur War.

On October 6, 1973, coinciding with Yom Kippur, the holiest day in the Jewish calendar, a coalition led by Egypt and Syria launched a coordinated attack on Israel. Egypt stormed across the Suez Canal, breaking Israel's defensive line, while Syria advanced into the Golan Heights.

The surprise was complete. Israel, with its guard down due to the holiday and a belief in its own invincibility post-1967, found itself scrambling. The early days of the war saw desperate battles and significant Israeli losses.

Yet, from this precarious position emerged tales of resilience. One anecdote revolves around a group of Israeli tank commanders in the Golan Heights, vastly outnumbered by Syrian forces. Despite their dire situation, they held their ground for three days, earning their stand the title of the "Valley of Tears." Their tenacity slowed the Syrian advance, allowing Israeli reinforcements to arrive.

As the days progressed, Israel managed to regroup and counterattack. With U.S. support in the form of an arms airlift, Israel not only repelled the invaders but advanced towards Damascus and encircled the Egyptian Third Army.

By October 25, when a ceasefire took effect, the war's landscape was transformed. While Israel could claim a military victory, it was a Pyrrhic one. The myth of Israeli invulnerability was shattered, leading to significant introspection and political upheaval in the country.

On the Arab side, the war restored a sense of pride, especially for Egypt. It paved the way for diplomatic initiatives, leading eventually to the Camp David Accords and a peace treaty between Israel and Egypt.

The Yom Kippur War, while lasting less than a month, had profound implications. It underscored the limitations of military might, the need for diplomacy, and the unpredictable, ever-shifting nature of Middle Eastern geopolitics.

Chapter 6: From Oslo to the Second Intifada

First Intifada and its Impact

The late 1980s witnessed a significant shift in the dynamics of the Palestinian-Israeli conflict. Away from the conventional wars of earlier decades, the struggle moved towards a popular uprising known as the First Intifada, or "shaking off" in Arabic.

The uprising began in December 1987 in the Gaza Strip when a traffic accident, involving an Israeli truck colliding with a car, resulted in the deaths of four Palestinians. What might have been dismissed as a tragic accident instead ignited simmering frustrations. The Palestinian territories, occupied by Israel since 1967, had experienced economic hardships, continuous settlement expansion, and daily interactions with the Israeli Defense Forces (IDF). The territories boiled over with spontaneous protests, strikes, and civil disobedience.

A poignant anecdote from this period involves a photograph that became emblematic of the Intifada. It depicted a Palestinian youth, with a sling in his hand, facing an Israeli tank. The image drew parallels to the biblical tale of David and Goliath, casting the Palestinians as the underdogs in their struggle against a mightier Israeli military.

For Israel, the Intifada was challenging not just in its physicality but its imagery. The Israeli military, which had faced conventional armies, was now confronted by stone-throwing youths and civilian protests. The optics of a well-equipped military facing off against largely unarmed civilians garnered international attention and often sympathy for the Palestinian cause.

The uprising culminated in major political shifts. The

Palestine Liberation Organization (PLO) adopted the Declaration of Independence in 1988, asserting a Palestinian state. This period also saw the PLO's gradual move towards recognizing Israel's right to exist and the acceptance of a two-state solution.

The First Intifada, lasting until 1993, altered the Palestinian-Israeli narrative. While it did not immediately result in a Palestinian state, it galvanized the Palestinian national identity and highlighted the need for a diplomatic solution, setting the stage for the Oslo Accords and subsequent peace efforts.

Oslo Accords

The early 1990s ushered in a renewed sense of optimism in the Middle East. Against the backdrop of the First Intifada and global geopolitical changes, including the end of the Cold War, the stage was set for what many hoped would be a historic peace agreement: the Oslo Accords.

The accords, named after the Norwegian capital where the initial secret negotiations took place, were signed in 1993 by representatives of Israel and the Palestine Liberation Organization (PLO). This was the first direct, face-to-face agreement between Israel and the PLO, and it aimed to pave the way for a comprehensive peace in the region.

At the heart of the accords was the principle of "land for peace." Israel would withdraw from Palestinian territories in phases, and in return, the Palestinians would recognize Israel's right to exist and renounce terrorism.

One memorable anecdote from this period is the iconic image from the White House lawn, where President Bill Clinton stood between Israeli Prime Minister Yitzhak Rabin and PLO

Chairman Yasser Arafat, encouraging them to shake hands. This symbolic gesture, broadcasted worldwide, encapsulated the hopes of countless individuals who dreamed of a lasting peace in the region.

Oslo led to the establishment of the Palestinian Authority, granting Palestinians self-rule in parts of the West Bank and Gaza Strip. However, the accords were not without their critics. Many Palestinians felt the agreement did not go far enough in ensuring a sovereign state, while some Israelis believed it compromised their security.

Indeed, as years passed, the optimism surrounding the Oslo Accords dimmed. Assassinations, notably that of Yitzhak Rabin in 1995, violence, and lack of trust on both sides eroded the promise of Oslo.

While the accords did not deliver the comprehensive peace many had hoped for, they remain a historic milestone, symbolizing the possibility of dialogue and the enduring hope for reconciliation between Israelis and Palestinians.

Second Intifada

The turn of the millennium saw the Palestinian-Israeli conflict escalate into a new wave of violence, known as the Second Intifada. Unlike the largely grassroots uprising of the first, this second iteration, spanning from 2000 to 2005, was marked by increased militarization and an even deeper toll on both societies.

The spark for the Second Intifada is often traced back to September 2000, when Ariel Sharon, the Israeli opposition leader at the time, made a controversial visit to the Temple Mount, or Haram al-Sharif, a site of immense religious significance for both Jews and Muslims. Perceived by many

Palestinians as a provocative gesture, it led to immediate protests, which rapidly escalated into a widespread uprising.

During this period, suicide bombings became a grimly familiar tactic, targeting Israeli buses, cafes, and public gatherings. Israel responded with military incursions, checkpoints, and targeted assassinations of militants. Civilian casualties were significant on both sides.

One haunting anecdote from this era involves a diary of a Palestinian girl named Farah, who chronicled her daily life amidst the chaos. An entry reads, "Today, there were no classes. Not because it's a holiday, but because of the nearby gunshots. We're used to it, but today was too close." This diary, later published, provided a glimpse into the life of ordinary individuals trapped in a conflict larger than themselves.

The Second Intifada, while similar in name to the first, was different in character. The Palestinian Authority, instead of being on the sidelines, was now more involved. The international community, too, was more deeply engaged, recognizing the urgency to curtail the violence.

The upsurge in violence gradually diminished by 2005, in part due to the construction of the Israeli West Bank barrier, fatigue on both sides, and renewed attempts at diplomacy. However, the scars of the Second Intifada, both physical and psychological, lingered, underscoring the challenges and complexities inherent in the path to a lasting peace.

Part II: Current State of Affairs

Chapter 7: The Complex Landscape

Palestinian Territories: West Bank and Gaza Strip

The Palestinian territories, comprised of the West Bank and Gaza Strip, are central to the Israeli-Palestinian conflict. Located to the east and west of Israel respectively, these territories are seen by Palestinians as the heartland of their future state.

The West Bank, dotted with ancient biblical sites, is landlocked and shares its longer border with Jordan. Its city of East Jerusalem, which Palestinians see as their future capital, holds religious significance for Muslims, Christians, and Jews alike.

The Gaza Strip, by contrast, is a narrow coastal enclave bordering Egypt. Dense and heavily populated, it's often described as one of the world's largest open-air prisons due to the restrictions on movement imposed by Israel and, to some extent, Egypt, citing security concerns.

An evocative anecdote comes from Sami, a Gazan fisherman, who once said, "The sea is the only open space in Gaza, but even there, we're trapped." He referred to the limited nautical miles off the Gazan coast where Palestinians can fish, a limit set by the Israeli navy for security reasons. Overstepping these bounds can lead to dire consequences, a reality Sami and other fishermen know too well.

Post-1967, Israel established settlements in both territories, deemed illegal under international law, although Israel disputes this. These settlements, coupled with security checkpoints and infrastructure, have fragmented the Palestinian landscape, impacting daily life, mobility, and prospects for statehood.

While the West Bank has seen relative stability in recent years under the Palestinian Authority's governance, Gaza, since 2007, has been under the control of Hamas, an Islamist militant group. This division has not only resulted in differing governance models but also in periodic conflicts between Hamas and Israel.

Understanding these territories is essential, as they encapsulate the broader dynamics of the Palestinian-Israeli issue: aspirations of statehood, challenges of occupation, security concerns, and the daily intricacies of lives lived in the midst of geopolitical turmoil.

Israeli Settlements and their Impacts

The Israeli settlements, communities established in territories occupied by Israel post-1967, stand as one of the most contentious aspects of the Palestinian-Israeli issue. Sprawling across the West Bank, East Jerusalem, and previously in the Gaza Strip (until 2005), these settlements are seen by many as symbols of Israeli occupation and as major obstacles to peace.

These communities, ranging from small outposts to large suburban towns, currently house several hundred thousand Israelis. Their establishment was driven by a mix of religious, nationalistic, and strategic motives. For some Israelis, these settlements represent a biblical birthright, a return to ancient Jewish lands. For others, they are seen as strategic buffers against potential attacks.

Yet, their expansion has been met with condemnation from the international community. The United Nations, for instance, views them as a breach of the Fourth Geneva

Convention, which prohibits an occupying power from transferring its own civilian population into the territory it occupies. Israel, however, challenges this interpretation.

For Palestinians, the impact of settlements is palpable. Beyond the symbolic affront to their statehood aspirations, settlements have tangible consequences. They fragment the West Bank, making the viability of a contiguous Palestinian state challenging. Moreover, the infrastructure accompanying these settlements, such as roads and security checkpoints, restrict Palestinian movement.

A telling anecdote comes from Hani, a Palestinian farmer, whose olive trees were cut down to make way for a settlement's expansion. "These trees were older than any treaty or argument," he remarked. "They were our family's legacy. In one day, it's all gone." Such stories underline the human cost of geopolitical maneuvers, highlighting how ordinary lives get caught in the crosshairs of larger political strategies.

It's worth noting that within Israel, settlements are a divisive issue. While some see them as essential for Israel's security and religious identity, others believe they compromise Israel's democratic character and peace prospects.

The settlements, with their profound impacts on the ground and their symbolic weight, underscore the intricate complexities that any peace process must navigate.

Jerusalem: A City Divided

Jerusalem, a mosaic of ancient alleyways and sacred shrines, has been the heart of religious and political tensions for centuries. Nestled in the Judean hills, its name evokes reverence across Jewish, Christian, and Muslim traditions, each of which has left an indelible mark on the city's tapestry.

For Jews, the Western Wall, a remnant of the ancient Second Temple, is a poignant symbol of millennia-old ties and divine promise. Christians, on the other hand, walk the Via Dolorosa, retracing Jesus's final steps to his crucifixion at the Church of the Holy Sepulchre. And for Muslims, the Al-Aqsa Mosque, with its gleaming golden dome, marks where the Prophet Muhammad is believed to have ascended to heaven.

This spiritual significance, however, is juxtaposed with the city's political divide. After the 1948 Arab-Israeli War, Jerusalem was split, with Israel controlling the west and Jordan the east, including the Old City. The 1967 Six-Day War saw Israel capturing East Jerusalem, a move not recognized internationally. Today, Israel claims the entire city as its "undivided" capital, while Palestinians envision East Jerusalem as the capital of their future state.

Amidst these political underpinnings, everyday life unfolds with its own complexities. An anecdote from Sarah, an Israeli shopkeeper, captures this essence. "I sell spices to everyone – Jewish, Muslim, Christian. The aromas don't know boundaries," she said. Yet, she added, "Outside my shop, it's a different story." Her observation paints a portrait of a city where divisions are palpable, but so are moments of shared humanity.

Tensions flare periodically around religious sites. For instance, the Temple Mount or Haram al-Sharif, revered by both Jews and Muslims, often becomes a flashpoint. Policies around access and control of these areas can ignite broader political and religious conflicts.

However, amidst the divisions, there are also tales of coexistence. Stories of neighbors celebrating each other's festivals, of shared taxis, and of interfaith dialogues that underline Jerusalem's potential as a city of peace.

Jerusalem, in essence, is both a city of profound divides and deep connections. Its layered history and spiritual resonance make it central to any discourse on the Palestinian-Israeli issue.

Chapter 8: Politics and Players

Palestinian Politics: Fatah, Hamas, and Beyond

Navigating the tumultuous landscape of Palestinian politics involves understanding the two dominant factions: Fatah and Hamas. These entities, while both representing Palestinian aspirations, are distinct in their ideologies, methodologies, and regional influences.

Fatah, the older of the two, was founded in the late 1950s by Yasser Arafat and other Palestinian expatriates. It emerged from the belief that Palestinians must lead their own struggle for liberation. In its early years, Fatah was primarily associated with guerrilla attacks against Israel but gradually moved towards diplomacy, notably becoming the dominant force within the Palestine Liberation Organization (PLO). By the 1990s, Arafat, as the leader of Fatah and the PLO, was negotiating directly with Israel, culminating in the Oslo Accords.

Hamas, on the other hand, was born in the 1980s during the First Intifada. Stemming from the Muslim Brotherhood, its foundation is deeply religious. Unlike Fatah, Hamas's charter originally rejected any permanent peace with Israel. Its rise was marked by a combination of social welfare initiatives for Palestinians and acts classified by many, including the U.S. and EU, as terrorism.

A poignant anecdote encapsulating their differences comes from Layla, a Palestinian teacher in Gaza: "Fatah taught us about liberation, while Hamas spoke of salvation. One talked politics, the other faith. Yet, for many of us, we simply yearned for a better tomorrow."

The rivalry between these two groups came to a head in 2006. In a surprising turn, Hamas won the Palestinian legislative elections. What followed was a period of internal strife, culminating in 2007 with Hamas seizing control of Gaza while Fatah remained dominant in the West Bank.

Beyond these two giants lie smaller factions, each with its influence. Groups like the Palestinian Islamic Jihad and the Popular Front for the Liberation of Palestine have played roles in shaping the region's dynamics.

Foreign powers, too, have stakes in this internal Palestinian politics. While Fatah historically drew support from countries like Saudi Arabia, Jordan, and the West, Hamas has been backed by Iran and Syria.

The divergences between Fatah and Hamas aren't merely political but also manifest in everyday Palestinian life, affecting governance, security, and international relations. Yet, both groups, despite their differences, symbolize the diverse tapestry of Palestinian resistance and aspiration. The future of Palestinian unity and statehood, many argue, rests on bridging the chasm between these two pivotal entities.

Israeli Political Landscape

Dive into Israel's political realm, and you'll find a spectrum as diverse as the land itself. This nation, young by historical standards, has a political tapestry interwoven with ideology, religion, and security concerns.

At its core, the Israeli political system is a parliamentary democracy, with the Knesset (parliament) at its heart. Members of the Knesset (MKs) are elected proportionally, leading to a multiparty system where coalition governments are the norm, given that no single party typically secures an outright majority.

Two significant political blocs have historically dominated the scene: the left-leaning Labor Party and the right-leaning Likud. The Labor Party, with its roots in the socialist Zionist movement, played a pivotal role in founding the state and was at the forefront of Israeli politics for its first few decades. Likud, founded in the 1970s, champions a more nationalist and conservative agenda.

Beyond these titans lie smaller parties, each with its distinctive stance. There are religious parties like Shas (Sephardic Orthodox) and United Torah Judaism (Ashkenazi Orthodox), which focus on Jewish religious issues. The Yisrael Beiteinu party, on the other hand, largely represents Russian-speaking immigrants. Additionally, Arab parties, such as the Joint List, represent the interests of Israel's Arab minority.

To illustrate the dynamics, consider an anecdote from Eli, a Tel Aviv cafe owner: "During election season, my cafe turns into a mini Knesset. You'll hear Yair arguing for a two-state solution, while Miriam, at the next table, worries about security and believes in a strong Israel. And then there's Ahmed, an Arab Israeli, voicing concerns about equality. It's a microcosm of our nation in one room."

Over the decades, the political pendulum has swung between these parties and blocs, influenced by events such as wars, Intifadas, peace negotiations, and shifts in global politics. The rise of new parties, often around charismatic leaders, is also a recurring theme.

A notable dynamic in Israeli politics is the significant role played by the defense establishment. Many top politicians, from Yitzhak Rabin to Ariel Sharon and Ehud Barak, transitioned from military careers, reflecting the nation's security-centric ethos.

The Israeli political landscape, with its intricacies, reflects the country's diverse population and the myriad challenges it faces. Understanding this spectrum is key to grasping the broader Israeli-Palestinian narrative and the potential paths to peace.

External Actors: Role of Neighboring Countries

The Israeli-Palestinian narrative, while deeply local at its core, cannot be understood without acknowledging the influence of its neighboring countries. The Middle East, a region renowned for its intricate political tapestry, has always cast long shadows over the Israeli-Palestinian saga.

Egypt, the most populous Arab nation, was the first to break ranks and recognize Israel following the Camp David Accords in 1978. This monumental peace treaty, overseen by U.S. President Jimmy Carter, ended decades of hostilities. It wasn't just about politics; it was personal. An anecdote recounts how Egyptian President Anwar Sadat, during his historic visit to Jerusalem, handed Israeli Prime Minister Menachem Begin a personal letter from an Egyptian child, expressing hope for peace. This symbolic gesture spoke volumes, emphasizing the shared human aspirations behind the political posturing.

Jordan, with its long shared border with both Israel and the West Bank, followed suit in 1994, signing a peace agreement with Israel. The Hashemite Kingdom has always had a special role, given its custodianship of Muslim holy sites in Jerusalem and its significant Palestinian population.

Syria remains in a state of technical war with Israel. The crux of their contention lies in the Golan Heights, a strategic plateau captured by Israel in the 1967 war. While there have been backchannel efforts at peace, these have consistently faltered, leaving the relationship tense and unresolved.

Lebanon has its own intricate ties with the Palestinian issue, particularly given the historical presence of Palestinian refugees and the emergence of Hezbollah, a Shiite militant group staunchly opposed to Israel. The Israel-Lebanon border has witnessed multiple conflicts, notably in 1982 and 2006, influenced by broader regional dynamics involving Iran and Syria.

Saudi Arabia and the Gulf states, while not direct neighbors, have played influential roles. Historically, they've supported Palestinian causes both politically and financially. However, recent years have seen a thaw in their relations with Israel, driven by mutual concerns over Iran and shared economic interests.

In this complex regional tableau, alliances aren't permanent, and enmities aren't eternal. The Palestinian issue often intertwines with broader regional politics, and shifts in one arena can ripple across others.

Understanding the roles and aspirations of these neighboring nations isn't just about geopolitics. It's about recognizing the broader Middle Eastern context in which the

Israeli-Palestinian story unfolds. As the region's nations grapple with their own challenges and transformations, their stances and relationships concerning the Palestinian-Israeli conflict continue to evolve.

Chapter 9: Daily Lives and Human Stories

Living Under Occupation: A Palestinian Perspective

Amidst the complex geopolitics, international treaties, and historical events that define the Israeli-Palestinian narrative, it's the personal stories of Palestinians living under occupation that resonate with the tangible realities of this long-standing conflict.

Occupation, for many Palestinians in the West Bank and East Jerusalem, is a daily experience. The landscape is interspersed with Israeli checkpoints, military bases, and settlements. Daily activities, like commuting to work or visiting a relative, often necessitate navigating these checkpoints. Such interactions with Israeli soldiers, for some, are routine, while for others, they're marked by tension or indignity.

The economic repercussions are palpable. With limited access to natural resources and severe restrictions on movement, economic growth has been stifled. Agriculture, once a pillar of Palestinian society, especially in the fertile Jordan Valley, faces challenges from land confiscations and limited water access.

Education too feels the strain. Palestinian students from the West Bank attending Al-Quds University in Jerusalem, for instance, often speak of the unpredictability in their commutes, never knowing how long a checkpoint delay might last.

Consider the story of Lina, a young Palestinian woman from Hebron. She recalls her childhood memory: "One evening, as my family gathered for dinner, Israeli soldiers knocked. They had come for a routine house search. My father, attempting to keep the atmosphere light for us kids, turned to the officer and joked, 'Would you like some falafel?' The officer, probably as weary as my dad, just nodded and moved on."

However, the emotional toll runs deeper than these daily inconveniences. Many Palestinians feel a profound sense of loss – loss of land, of autonomy, and of national identity. The older generation mourns homes left behind, while the youth grapple with their place and identity in a fractured homeland.

It's also crucial to note that the occupation is not monolithic in its experience. Gazans, living under a blockade and having faced several military confrontations, endure a markedly different reality than their West Bank counterparts.

Yet, amidst these challenges, resilience shines. Whether it's through art, literature, education, or peaceful protests, Palestinians continuously assert their identity and aspirations for a free and dignified existence.

Understanding the Palestinian perspective is more than an exercise in empathy; it's integral to grasping the depth and nuances of the Israeli-Palestinian conflict. For beyond the headlines and the political maneuverings, it's the daily lived experiences that most poignantly illuminate the ramifications of this enduring dispute.

Living with Security Concerns: An Israeli Perspective

For Israelis, the narrative of their nation is intricately woven with the tenets of survival, resilience, and security. Amidst the multifaceted backdrop of the Middle East, where geopolitical complexities are a constant, security concerns have profoundly shaped the Israeli psyche.

In the urban fabric of cities like Tel Aviv and Jerusalem, bomb shelters are as ubiquitous as playgrounds. These concrete enclosures, often painted with vibrant murals or used as community centers during times of peace, stand as silent reminders of the potential threats that lurk beyond moments of calm. Schools routinely conduct drills, training children on what to do during missile attacks, a practice that might seem alien in many parts of the world but is standard in Israel.

The mandatory military service, a rite of passage for most Israeli youth, is both a means of defense and a melting pot of Israeli society. Here, young adults from diverse backgrounds come together, their experiences shaping both personal trajectories and the nation's ethos.

There's an anecdote about a young Israeli mother, Tamar, shopping in a bustling market in Jerusalem. Suddenly, a siren blares, indicating an incoming missile. As people rush for cover, Tamar, cradling her infant, finds herself sheltered by strangers in a nearby store. Once the threat subsides and she steps out, she murmurs a thank-you, only to be met with a knowing nod—a silent acknowledgment of a shared experience that binds the community.

Yet, it's not just the overt military threats that weigh on the Israeli consciousness. It's also the more insidious fears: the fear of a suicide bomber in a crowded cafe, a knife-wielding assailant at a bus stop, or the random rocket launched from the Gaza Strip.

These concerns have spurred innovations in security and intelligence, with Israel emerging as a global leader in these sectors. The nation's technological prowess, in many ways, has been driven by the imperative of security.

However, it would be a disservice to reduce the Israeli experience solely to its security dilemmas. Many Israelis yearn for lasting peace and understand the costs of continuous conflict. The peace rallies, the dialogues between communities, and various coexistence projects all underscore a desire to find a solution that ensures security while also recognizing the rights and aspirations of Palestinians.

To truly comprehend the Israeli-Palestinian conflict, one must juxtapose the very real security concerns of Israelis with the aspirations and challenges faced by Palestinians. It's this duality, complex and often heart-wrenching, that underscores the challenge of finding a path forward to mutual peace and coexistence.

Stories of Collaboration and Coexistence

Amidst the tapestry of conflict that characterizes the Israeli-Palestinian narrative, there are threads of hope woven by individuals and communities striving for understanding, collaboration, and coexistence. These stories, while often overshadowed by more sensational headlines, capture the spirit of human resilience and the enduring hope for peace.

One notable initiative is the "Hand in Hand" schools. Here, Jewish and Arab children are educated together, using both Arabic and Hebrew, fostering understanding from a young age. The curriculum is designed not only to teach math, science, and literature but also to instill mutual respect and a shared sense of community. It's a space where festivals from both cultures are celebrated with equal fervor, where differences are acknowledged, and commonalities celebrated.

Take, for example, the story of Amir and Sami. Amir, a Jewish boy, and Sami, an Arab, met in first grade at a Hand in Hand school. Over the years, their bond deepened. Sami recounts a Hanukkah evening when he and Amir lit the menorah together, and in return, Amir joined Sami's family for an Iftar meal during Ramadan. Their families, once wary, found camaraderie in shared meals and celebrations, epitomizing the potential of interpersonal relationships to bridge divides.

Another beacon of collaboration is the Arava Institute, where environmental challenges, transcending political borders, bring together Israeli, Palestinian, and Jordanian students. Here, under the vast desert sky, these future environmentalists work on shared problems, recognizing that nature, in its vastness, does not adhere to man-made boundaries.

The city of Haifa, often dubbed the "City of Coexistence," offers a glimpse into the harmonious life possible between Jewish and Arab residents. In this bustling port city, mixed neighborhoods, shared businesses, and cultural exchanges are not the exception but the norm.

However, these stories of collaboration aren't limited to formal initiatives. They are found in shared taxis, where conversations flow effortlessly in mixed languages, in marketplaces where Jewish and Arab traders exchange goods and banter alike, and in the music collaborations that blend Eastern and Western tones.

Yet, while these tales of coexistence provide hope, they also highlight the potential that remains largely untapped. They serve as a reminder that beneath the layers of politics and history, there exists a simple, human desire to connect, to understand, and to coexist.

These stories challenge the monolithic narratives of perpetual animosity, showcasing the transformative power of human connection. They whisper a potent message: if given a chance, bridges can be built, not just between territories, but hearts.

Chapter 10: Roadblocks to Peace

Issues of Refugees and Right of Return

The Palestinian refugee issue is one of the most emotive and contentious aspects of the Israeli-Palestinian conflict. Rooted deeply in the historical narrative of both peoples, it embodies the Palestinian sense of displacement and longing and poses significant challenges to the demographic and security concerns of Israel.

In the aftermath of the 1948 Arab-Israeli war, vast numbers of Palestinians fled or were expelled from their homes. These individuals and their descendants, now numbering in the millions, predominantly reside in Jordan, Lebanon, Syria, the West Bank, and the Gaza Strip. Life in refugee camps, meant initially as temporary settlements, has for many become a multi-generational experience, marked by poverty, lack of opportunities, and a yearning for a homeland often seen only in the stories of elders.

The "Right of Return," a term echoing through years of negotiations, is a Palestinian demand that these refugees should have the option to return to the homes they left behind in what is now Israel. Rooted in the United Nations General Assembly Resolution 194, it has become a powerful symbol of the Palestinian national narrative.

To elucidate the depth of this sentiment, consider the tale of Fatima, an elderly Palestinian woman from a refugee camp in Lebanon. Clutching the rusted key to her family home in Haifa—a home she had to flee as a child—she speaks of her dream to let her grandchildren see the verdant orchard she played in, even if just once. To her, and many like her, the key isn't a mere relic but a testament to an unbroken bond with the land.

For Israel, the challenge is multifaceted. A massive influx of Palestinian refugees poses substantial demographic implications for a state built as a homeland for the Jewish people. Additionally, there are concerns about potential security threats and the societal integration of returning individuals.

While there's no easy solution, various propositions have emerged over the years, ranging from limited return paired with compensation, resettlement in a future Palestinian state, or third-country absorption. The key lies in finding a solution that addresses the genuine grievances of the Palestinian refugees while respecting the demographic and security considerations of Israel.

This issue, like many others in this intricate conflict, exemplifies the balance of justice, memory, and practicality. The path forward will require innovative thinking, mutual recognition of historical wounds, and a commitment to crafting a shared future.

Borders and Security Concerns

In the story of the Israeli-Palestinian conflict, the topic of borders is not just about lines on a map. It's a tale of shifting sands, both literally and metaphorically, that have seen empires, nations, and peoples rise and fall, often with the whisper of olive trees and the echo of ancient cities as silent witnesses.

Following the 1967 Six-Day War, Israel took control of the West Bank, Gaza Strip, and East Jerusalem. These territories are often referred to as the "Occupied Territories" and have since been the subject of intense negotiation. The question is: Where should the lines be drawn to ensure a viable Palestinian state while also ensuring the security of Israel?

The tale of Yitzhak, an Israeli farmer, sheds a light on the personal resonance of this issue. Yitzhak's farm, passed down from his grandparents, lies close to the Green Line, the armistice boundary set in 1949. From his fields, he can see a nearby Palestinian village. Over the years, he's built a rapport with some of its residents, but he also recalls tense nights when rockets were fired. "It's a strange thing," he muses, "to see your neighbor's home from your backyard and not know if the next day will bring a wave or a warning siren."

Security is paramount for Israel. The West Bank's elevation provides a strategic depth, as its highlands overlook Israel's coastal plain where the majority of its population resides. Any future Palestinian state's borders, Israel argues, must ensure that it doesn't become a launchpad for attacks, be it by rockets, tunnels, or other means. The Jordan Valley, often referred to as Israel's "security belt," is deemed by many in Israel as crucial for its defense, acting as a buffer against potential threats from the east.

For Palestinians, a state that's territorially contiguous and economically viable is essential. Enclaves or isolated patches of land wouldn't just be challenging to govern but would also not meet the aspirations of a people yearning for self-determination. The 2002 Arab Peace Initiative, for instance, proposed a return to the pre-1967 borders with mutually agreed upon land swaps.

Security arrangements, border crossings, and the nature of any international presence are among the myriad of details that have been topics of negotiations. The challenge remains: crafting borders that satisfy Palestinian aspirations for statehood and Israel's security concerns.

As the chapter closes, it's worth noting that borders aren't just about security or statehood. They're about lives, stories, and memories intertwined with every inch of the land, waiting for a future where they can coexist in harmony.

Religious and Cultural Sensitivities

In the heart of the Middle East, where history meets prophecy, the Israeli-Palestinian conflict is deeply intertwined with religious sentiments and cultural memories. The land, often called "Holy," is sacred to three major world religions: Judaism, Christianity, and Islam.

For Jews, it's the land of their forefathers, where the Temple of Solomon once stood and where the Western Wall, the last remaining part of the Second Temple, remains a poignant symbol of their millennia-long connection. The whisper of prayers at the Wall tells stories of exiles, returns, and an unbreakable bond with the land.

Muslims revere the Al-Aqsa Mosque in Jerusalem as the site from where Prophet Muhammad is believed to have ascended to heaven during his Night Journey. The melodious call to prayer, echoing through the ancient stone alleyways, is a reminder of the deep Islamic roots in the region.

Christians see the Holy Land as the backdrop to the life of Jesus Christ. The Church of the Holy Sepulchre, believed by many to be the site of Jesus' crucifixion and resurrection, attracts pilgrims from around the world.

Yet, with these overlapping sacred geographies come inevitable sensitivities. Take, for instance, Sarah, a Jewish woman who once shared a touching story of finding an old family menorah (a seven-branched candelabrum) that had been lost during a tumultuous period. To her, it wasn't just an artifact but a symbol of her family's unbroken chain in this land. Meanwhile, Mahmoud, a Palestinian, cherishes a key, an emblem of the home his grandparents left behind and hope to return to. Both artifacts, while deeply personal, are emblematic of the broader cultural and religious tapestry of the region.

As this chapter unfolds, it's evident that the land is not just about politics or territory; it's a mosaic of beliefs, stories, and dreams, each thread as significant as the other, demanding understanding and respect.

Part III: The U.S. Involvement and Implications

Chapter 11: American Diplomacy and the Peace Process

U.S. Role in Middle East Peace Talks

In the midst of the Middle East's intricate politics, the United States has been a key player, particularly in Israeli-Palestinian peace talks. Since the mid-20th century, the U.S. has taken on the mantle of mediator, aiming to bring both sides to a negotiated settlement.

The 1978 Camp David Accords marked a significant U.S.-brokered agreement between Egypt and Israel, where President Jimmy Carter played a pivotal role. While this deal didn't directly address Palestinian concerns, it set a precedent for American involvement.

In the 1990s, under President Bill Clinton's leadership, the U.S. facilitated the Oslo Accords – landmark agreements between Israel and the Palestine Liberation Organization (PLO). These accords marked the first mutual recognition between the two parties.

Yet, the road to peace is riddled with challenges. Picture a moment at Camp David in 2000: Clinton, Israeli Prime Minister Ehud Barak, and Palestinian leader Yasser Arafat, locked in intense discussions. Despite thirteen days of negotiations, they couldn't reach a final agreement. Clinton later recalled the weight of that moment, remarking on the layers of historical and emotional complexities.

Subsequent U.S. administrations have made varied attempts to broker peace, with each bringing its own approach. The Trump administration, for example, unveiled a "Peace to Prosperity" plan, which garnered mixed reactions.

While the U.S. has often been seen as leaning towards Israel due to strong political, military, and cultural ties, it has always maintained a stance that a two-state solution is the best outcome for peace.

Behind the high-profile meetings and official statements lie countless untold stories. Like that of a young American diplomat who, during a stay in Jerusalem, would have informal evening chats with local Israeli and Palestinian youth. In their shared dreams and fears, he saw the raw human essence of the conflict, beyond the realm of politics.

The U.S. involvement in the Middle East peace talks underscores the global significance of the Israeli-Palestinian issue. And as history has shown, while achieving lasting peace is an uphill task, the quest for it remains undeterred.

Major Initiatives: From Camp David to Recent Times

Spanning several decades, the Israeli-Palestinian conflict has seen numerous international initiatives to forge peace. Each one has been a testament to the world's hope for resolution, even in the face of repeated setbacks.

The Camp David Accords (1978) is often hailed as a remarkable peace endeavor, facilitated by U.S. President Jimmy Carter. This was not an Israeli-Palestinian agreement, but rather one between Egypt and Israel. Still, its significance lies in the fact that it marked the first peace treaty between Israel and an Arab nation. Imagine the serene Camp David setting, where leaders of once-warring nations shared meals and, in one light moment, even watched a movie together. Such glimpses of camaraderie provided hope.

Fast forward to the 1990s, and the Oslo Accords come into focus. Envisaged in secret in Norway, this agreement marked the first official mutual recognition between Israel and the Palestine Liberation Organization (PLO). The iconic image from this period is the White House lawn handshake between Yitzhak Rabin and Yasser Arafat, with a beaming Bill Clinton standing between them.

The 2000 Camp David Summit, though it failed to produce a final agreement, highlighted the intricacies of the conflict. It was here that the thorny issues of Jerusalem, refugees, and final borders were discussed at length.

The Roadmap for Peace (2003) was another significant initiative, introduced by the U.S., in collaboration with Russia, the European Union, and the United Nations. Its goal was clear: a two-state solution.

2007 saw the Annapolis Conference, hosted by U.S. President George W. Bush. While it rekindled the commitment to a two-state solution, concrete outcomes remained elusive.

In recent times, initiatives like the Abraham Accords (2020) shifted the landscape. While not directly addressing the Israeli-Palestinian issue, these agreements normalized relations between Israel and several Arab states.

Anecdotal stories from these negotiations humanize the process. At one of the many tense dinners during the Oslo negotiations, a Norwegian official broke the ice by humorously comparing the lengthy peace talks to the slow-cooked traditional fish dish of lutefisk, which takes days to prepare. Both sides laughed, a reminder that sometimes, diplomacy benefits from shared human moments.

These major peace initiatives, each unique, have collectively shaped the landscape of the conflict. They highlight global aspirations for peace and the myriad challenges in attaining it.

Successes, Failures, and Controversies

In the Israeli-Palestinian narrative, successes and failures often intertwine, with controversies seldom far behind.

Starting with successes, the Oslo Accords of the 1990s were groundbreaking. Beyond mutual recognition, they established the Palestinian Authority and gave Palestinians limited self-governance in parts of the West Bank and Gaza. The iconic handshake on the White House lawn between leaders of long-hostile sides was emblematic of this breakthrough.

However, where there's light, shadows are cast. The Oslo Accords had their pitfalls. Extremists on both sides vehemently opposed the concessions made. Yitzhak Rabin, the Israeli Prime Minister who dared to dream of peace, was assassinated by a Jewish extremist in 1995. The dream had its price.

Further success came with the Israeli withdrawal from Gaza in 2005. Here was Israel, dismantling all its settlements in the strip. Yet, this unilateral move didn't usher in peace. Instead, Hamas took control of Gaza, and the territory became a launchpad for rockets into Israel, leading to recurring conflicts.

One cannot overlook the controversies tied to the broader conflict. The settlements Israel has built in the West Bank are a major sticking point. International law views them as illogal, but Iorael dioputoo thio.

Then there's the security barrier – a wall in some sections – erected by Israel in the West Bank. Israel insists it's essential for security, but Palestinians see it as a land grab and a physical manifestation of their isolation.

One intriguing story amidst the often grim tales of conflict revolves around an unlikely hero: a strawberry. In certain periods, under cooperation initiatives, Israeli experts trained Palestinian farmers in Gaza to grow high-quality strawberries. These berries made their way to European markets, a sweet fruit of collaboration, standing out in a field often bitter with hostilities.

Peace initiatives, like the Camp David talks, the Roadmap for Peace, and more, have oscillated between hope and despair. Each initiative has had its staunch defenders and critics.

The trajectory of the Israeli-Palestinian narrative is like the rugged landscape of the region itself – with its peaks of hope and deep valleys of disappointment. Yet, just as rivers persistently carve their way through these terrains, the quest for a lasting resolution continues, undeterred.

Chapter 12: U.S.-Israeli Relations

Historical Ties and Shared Values

The bond between the U.S. and Israel has its roots deep in the tapestry of history, interwoven with shared values and strategic interests. Beyond geopolitics, the relationship is steeped in a mutual appreciation of democratic ideals, an admiration for entrepreneurial spirit, and a commitment to freedom.

In the early days of Israel's statehood, President Harry Truman recognized the new nation just eleven minutes after its declaration, marking the onset of a steadfast alliance. But why such prompt support? Some argue it was Truman's understanding of the Holocaust's horrors; others believe it was the Biblical tales of Israel that resonated deeply with America's Christian ethos.

One such story tells of Golda Meir, Israel's then-ambassador, meeting with Truman. She handed him a gift - a Torah scroll. The President, moved, said, "I had this book for a long time." This anecdote isn't just about shared religious texts; it underscores the depth of spiritual and moral connections.

Fast forward, and the ties have only strengthened. Both nations, having emerged from the crucibles of conflict, value the principles of democracy: freedom of speech, religion, and the press. These shared democratic values are not just on paper; they manifest in day-to-day life, in bustling Israeli markets and American town hall meetings alike.

Economic innovation and entrepreneurial zeal further bolster this relationship. Silicon Valley's tech giants often find their counterparts in Tel Aviv, the world's second most important tech hub. From cybersecurity to drip irrigation, the collaboration has led to solutions that address global challenges.

However, shared values also come with shared threats. Both nations, in their pursuit of democracy, have faced threats to their existence and security. This mutual understanding of what's at stake has often led to joint efforts, be it intelligence sharing or military cooperation.

Yet, like any relationship, it's not without its critiques or complexities. Over the decades, policy differences have occasionally surfaced. But the bedrock of shared values—of freedom, democracy, and a pioneering spirit—continually brings the two nations back together, striving for a better future for their people.

In reflecting on this bond, it's evident that while strategic interests might fluctuate, deep-rooted values endure. It's a reminder that nations, at their core, are not just about land or borders, but about shared stories, mutual respect, and the hopes of their citizens.

Military and Economic Cooperation

The linchpins of the U.S.-Israeli relationship have often been anchored in military and economic partnerships. These cooperations, initiated from shared strategic interests and mutual respect, have matured into vital elements for both nations' prosperity and security.

In the realm of military ties, U.S. assistance to Israel began modestly with a $100 million loan in 1949. However, the 1967 Six-Day War became a turning point. The U.S. witnessed Israel's strategic value in the Middle East, and military aid intensified. Since then, Israel has been a leading recipient of U.S. foreign military aid, receiving advanced defense systems, aircraft, and intelligence support.

One notable example of this cooperation is the Iron Dome, a missile defense system that has been crucial in intercepting incoming rockets. Developed by Israeli firms with significant U.S. financial support, the Iron Dome has not only saved countless lives but also symbolizes the fruits of bilateral military research and cooperation.

Economically, both nations have been intrinsically intertwined since the signing of the U.S.-Israel Free Trade Agreement in 1985 – the first FTA the U.S. ever signed. This agreement set the stage for exponential growth in bilateral trade, with technology, agriculture, and pharmaceuticals being focal points.

A charming anecdote emerges from this partnership. In the late 1980s, an Israeli company introduced a revolutionary new product to the U.S. market: drip irrigation. Skeptical American farmers jokingly referred to it as "that spaghetti tube thing." But when they witnessed its water-saving potential, especially in arid regions, it swiftly became an essential tool. Today, this "spaghetti tube" stands testament to the innovative collaborations springing from economic ties.

Investment has also been a two-way street. American tech giants have research centers in Israel, and Israeli startups frequently turn to U.S. markets for expansion. This synergy isn't just about business; it's about shared values of innovation and entrepreneurship.

In sum, the U.S. and Israel's military and economic partnerships are not just transactional. They encapsulate mutual admiration, trust, and a shared vision for a safer, more prosperous world. Whether it's a cutting-edge defense system or a simple "spaghetti tube," these collaborations narrate a story of two nations working hand in hand, driving progress.

American Jewish Community and its Influence

America's Jewish community, estimated at over 6 million, is a mosaic of traditions, cultures, and influences. While making up just about 2% of the U.S. population, its impact on American politics, culture, and particularly on U.S.-Israeli relations, is profound.

Historically, Jewish immigrants to America, primarily from Eastern Europe in the late 19th and early 20th centuries, sought refuge from persecution and sought a better life. These early immigrants laid the foundation of a vibrant Jewish American community, establishing synagogues, cultural institutions, and philanthropic organizations.

Fast forward to the present, and the American Jewish community is multifaceted. While religious traditions remain vital, many Jews also identify culturally or ethically, contributing to a broad spectrum of beliefs and practices. Regardless of these internal differences, there's a consistent

71

theme of community engagement, particularly in politics and social justice.

The establishment of Israel in 1948 invoked a sense of pride among American Jews. The U.S.-Israel bond has often been strengthened by Jewish-American advocacy groups. Organizations like AIPAC (American Israel Public Affairs Committee) have played significant roles in shaping American policy towards Israel, lobbying for foreign aid and fostering bilateral ties.

However, it's essential to remember that the American Jewish perspective on Israel is diverse. While many passionately support Israel, the ways in which that support manifests can differ. For instance, J Street, another influential group, advocates for a two-state solution and has occasionally critiqued Israeli policies.

Here's an intriguing anecdote: In the 1970s, a group of American Jewish activists, alarmed by the plight of Soviet Jewry, launched a campaign using an unconventional method – wearing bracelets engraved with the names of Refuseniks, Jews who were denied permission to emigrate from the USSR. The campaign gained significant attention and was a precursor to the broader movement that eventually saw thousands of Soviet Jews immigrate to Israel and the U.S. This grassroots effort underscores the American Jewish community's commitment to global Jewish causes.

In the realms of culture, arts, and academia, Jewish Americans have made significant contributions, enriching America's tapestry. Names like Bob Dylan, Ruth Bader Ginsburg, and Steven Spielberg are not just Jewish-American icons; they're American legends.

In summation, the American Jewish community, with its diverse voices, has left an indelible mark on the nation's socio-political fabric. Their advocacy for Israel, commitment to social justice, and vast cultural contributions embody a rich legacy and an influential presence in the American story.

Chapter 13: U.S.-Palestinian Relations

The American Perspective on Palestinian Governance

America's involvement in the Middle East, especially the Israeli-Palestinian conflict, is storied and multifaceted. Amidst the complexities, U.S. views on Palestinian governance have oscillated between cautious optimism and concerns.

Historically, the U.S. recognized the Palestine Liberation Organization (PLO) as the representative of the Palestinian people in the late 1980s. This was a significant shift, heralding a period of diplomacy, as the PLO renounced terrorism and acknowledged Israel's right to exist. The 1990s' Oslo Accords, brokered with U.S. involvement, symbolized hope for a two-state solution, with the establishment of the Palestinian Authority (PA) as a step towards Palestinian self-governance.

However, challenges have marred the journey. The emergence of Hamas, a group the U.S. designates as a terrorist organization, after its victory in the 2006 Palestinian legislative elections, split Palestinian territories into two entities: Hamas-controlled Gaza and the PA-controlled West Bank. The U.S. stance, aligning with that of Israel and the European Union, was clear: no official engagement with Hamas unless it recognizes Israel, renounces violence, and adheres to past agreements.

A noteworthy anecdote paints the picture of these complex dynamics: In 2007, amidst the backdrop of escalating tensions between Fatah and Hamas, U.S. Secretary of State Condoleezza Rice embarked on a Middle East tour. In a meeting with Palestinian President Mahmoud Abbas, she was presented with a unique gift – a Palestinian scarf decorated with the flags of the U.S. and Palestine. This simple gesture, amidst turbulent times, signified the hope for unity, understanding, and peace, reflecting the nuances of U.S.-Palestinian interactions.

Over the years, the U.S. has consistently expressed concerns over issues like corruption within the PA, lack of press freedom, and human rights abuses. Nevertheless, America has been a significant donor to the Palestinian territories, offering aid for development, governance, and security reforms. This aid, however, has often been a double-edged sword, subjected to cuts and conditions based on shifting political landscapes.

To conclude, the American perspective on Palestinian governance, while grounded in the hopes of a stable, peaceful, and democratic Palestinian state, remains entwined in the broader, often tumultuous, landscape of the Israeli-Palestinian conflict. With each new U.S. administration and changing dynamics on the ground, this perspective continues to evolve, balancing diplomacy with strategic interests.

Aid, Diplomacy, and Engagement

The U.S. relationship with the Palestinians, while complex, can be characterized by three defining pillars: aid, diplomacy, and engagement. Each has evolved over time, reflecting the shifts in geopolitics and the intricate dynamics of the Middle East.

Aid: Since the Oslo Accords, the U.S. has channeled billions in financial assistance to the Palestinians, primarily through the U.S. Agency for International Development (USAID). This aid has been directed at infrastructure projects, health, education, and governance reforms. A notable project is the construction of roads and schools in the West Bank, often bearing plaques acknowledging U.S. contributions.

However, aid has always been more than just philanthropy. It's been a tool for encouraging peace negotiations and fostering stability. In some instances, funding has been withheld or cut, reflecting U.S. concerns about Palestinian actions or to pressurize Palestinian leadership into negotiations.

Diplomacy: U.S. diplomatic efforts with the Palestinians have often been conducted in tandem with peace process initiatives involving Israel. From the Madrid Conference to the Oslo Accords and beyond, the U.S. has played a central role. Yet, it's been a path filled with peaks and valleys. Triumphs like the iconic handshake between Yitzhak Rabin and Yasser Arafat on the White House lawn in 1993 are countered by periods of stagnation or regression.

An anecdote that captures the spirit of U.S. diplomacy involves President Bill Clinton at the 2000 Camp David Summit. Frustrated by the lack of progress, he reportedly told both Palestinian and Israeli leaders, "Don't come to Camp David and pretend. If you can't take the heat, stay out of the kitchen." It was a reflection of both the immense challenges and the U.S. determination to broker peace.

Engagement: Beyond formal diplomacy, U.S. engagement has also focused on grassroots initiatives. These involve exchanges, educational programs, and collaborations aiming to foster mutual understanding between Palestinians and Americans. Organizations like the Middle East Partnership

Initiative (MEPI) have championed programs that empower young Palestinian leaders, entrepreneurs, and civil society.

In conclusion, the U.S.-Palestinian relationship, shaped by aid, diplomacy, and engagement, is nuanced and multifaceted. While political headlines often capture moments of tension or breakthroughs, beneath them lies a rich tapestry of efforts, hopes, and human stories that continue to define the journey towards a lasting peace.

Challenges in Balancing Relations with Israel

Navigating the complex waters of the Middle East has always presented the U.S. with a balancing act, especially when fostering relations with both Israel and the Palestinians. The historical, strategic, and moral imperatives driving the close U.S.-Israeli bond often pose challenges for American diplomats seeking a just solution for the Palestinians.

Strategic Alliances: Israel is undeniably one of America's closest allies in the region. Rooted in shared democratic values, this relationship has been fortified by mutual security concerns, especially regarding regional instability and threats posed by certain actors in the Middle East. As such, the U.S. commitment to Israel's security often takes center stage, sometimes at the expense of Palestinian aspirations.

Domestic Politics: American political dynamics play a significant role. Israel enjoys broad bipartisan support in Congress. Moreover, influential lobby groups, such as the American Israel Public Affairs Committee (AIPAC), have a notable impact on U.S. foreign policy. While there's a growing voice advocating for Palestinian rights, the scales have historically tilted towards Israel.

An intriguing anecdote here involves President Dwight D. Eisenhower, who, during the 1956 Suez Crisis, exerted pressure on Britain, France, and Israel to withdraw from Egyptian territories. He famously said, "We must not allow ourselves to be forced into the position of choosing between one friend in the region and another." It underscores the eternal tightrope the U.S. treads in the region.

Public Perception and Media: The American public's perception of the conflict is largely influenced by media representation. Often, the complexities get lost, leading to polarized views. Ensuring balanced, nuanced reporting remains a challenge, with both sides of the conflict feeling misunderstood or misrepresented.

Diplomatic Nuances: U.S. attempts to act as an honest broker in peace talks are frequently scrutinized. The Palestinians have, at times, expressed concerns about the U.S.'s ability to be impartial, given its close ties with Israel. This sentiment was particularly evident following the U.S. recognition of Jerusalem as Israel's capital in 2017.

In summary, while the U.S. strives for a peaceful resolution between Israelis and Palestinians, its longstanding alliance with Israel presents challenges. Balancing the commitment to Israeli security with the legitimate aspirations of the Palestinians requires diplomacy, understanding, and, above all, a dedication to the ideals of justice and coexistence.

Chapter 14: Potential Dangers and American Stakes

The Broader Middle East and American Interests

The Middle East has long been a crucible of global geopolitics, its strategic importance elevated by oil reserves, trade routes, and historic cultural intersections. For the U.S., interests in the Middle East have been multifaceted, shaped by concerns over energy security, regional stability, and alliances formed in the shadows of the Cold War.

Oil and Energy Security: The discovery of oil in the Middle East in the 20th century transformed the region into a global energy powerhouse. Ensuring the free flow of this oil became a cornerstone of U.S. foreign policy. As President Franklin D. Roosevelt once whispered to British Prime Minister Winston Churchill regarding Saudi Arabia, "It's a matter of getting its oil." This underscored the economic importance of the Middle East to Western powers.

Cold War Dynamics: The geopolitical chessboard of the Cold War saw the U.S. and Soviet Union vying for influence in the Middle East. America sought to counter Soviet advances by forging alliances, exemplified by the Baghdad Pact of 1955. The region became a hotbed of proxy confrontations, each superpower aligning with states based on ideological leanings.

A brief, intriguing anecdote: In 1957, fearing communist expansion in the Middle East, President Dwight D. Eisenhower articulated the "Eisenhower Doctrine," pledging U.S. economic and military assistance to Middle Eastern countries resisting communist aggression. However, the actual enemy many Middle Eastern states were concerned about was not communism, but rather regional rivalries.

Terrorism and Regional Stability: Post-Cold War, the U.S. focus shifted to countering terrorism and ensuring regional stability. The 9/11 attacks galvanized U.S. efforts to combat extremist ideologies, leading to military interventions in Afghanistan and Iraq.

Israel and the Palestinian Issue: The Israeli-Palestinian conflict remains a central concern. While the U.S. maintains a close relationship with Israel, it acknowledges the need for a just resolution to Palestinian aspirations, believing that peace here can influence broader regional stability.

Nuclear Concerns: The potential proliferation of nuclear weapons, especially concerning Iran's nuclear ambitions, has been a significant focus. The U.S. seeks to prevent any destabilization that a nuclear-armed state might bring to the region.

Rise of New Powers: The emergence of China and Russia as influential players, vying for footholds in the Middle East, brings fresh challenges for American diplomacy.

In essence, the Middle East remains crucial to American strategic interests. Navigating its complexities requires a deft understanding of historical legacies, evolving geopolitical dynamics, and the aspirations of its diverse peoples.

The Dangers of Continued Conflict

For decades, the Palestinian-Israeli conflict has simmered and occasionally boiled over, affecting not only the lives of those directly involved but resonating globally. The prolonged nature of this dispute poses significant dangers, some evident and others lurking subtly beneath the surface.

Humanitarian Toll: At the forefront are the immeasurable human costs. Lives lost, families torn apart, children growing up in the shadows of walls and checkpoints. The trauma, both psychological and physical, ripples through generations. Gazan children, for instance, who have lived through multiple conflicts, carry the scars of war, affecting their mental health and future prospects.

A brief anecdote: In the West Bank, a Palestinian olive farmer once remarked that planting an olive tree is an act of defiance and hope. His trees, some older than the conflict itself, stand as silent witnesses to history, their roots delving deep, even as skirmishes threaten their existence.

Regional Instability: The Palestinian-Israeli conflict perpetually risks igniting a broader regional conflagration. Neighboring countries, many with Palestinian refugee populations and their own domestic challenges, can be pulled into the fray, destabilizing an already volatile Middle East.

Global Security: The dispute has provided fodder for extremist ideologies. Radical groups exploit the unresolved conflict, recruiting sympathizers by highlighting perceived injustices. This radicalization poses a threat well beyond the region's borders.

Economic Strain: Sustained conflict drains resources. Israel's defense budget, vital given its security concerns, limits funds available for education, health, and social welfare. For Palestinians, blockades and restrictions cripple economic prospects, leading to unemployment and poverty.

Diminishing Prospects for Peace: With each flare-up, mistrust deepens. Narratives become further entrenched, and the space for dialogue shrinks. A Palestinian teacher and an Israeli businessman, both yearning for peace, might find their hopes dashed with each rocket fired or settlement expanded.

Global Diplomacy and Reputation: The conflict often places allies in precarious positions. Countries, including the U.S., find themselves walking a diplomatic tightrope, supporting Israel's security while advocating for Palestinian rights. This balancing act can strain international relations.

In conclusion, the dangers of the continued Palestinian-Israeli conflict are profound and manifold. It's a vortex that consumes hopes, dreams, and resources, underscoring the urgent need for a resolution that ensures dignity, security, and justice for all.

Implications for American National Security and Global Peace

The Palestinian-Israeli conflict, while regional in its geography, casts a long shadow on the global stage, with particular implications for American national security and the broader pursuit of international peace.

Fueling Extremism: One of the most direct implications for American security is how the conflict provides rhetorical ammunition for extremist groups. The perception that the U.S. is siding with Israel can be exploited by radicals to foster anti-American sentiments, increasing recruitment and support for extremist factions.

Diplomatic Strain: The U.S.'s position on the conflict frequently places it at odds with international peers, especially in multilateral forums like the UN. This can hinder collaborations on other global issues, from climate change to counter-terrorism efforts.

Threats to Allies: America's Middle Eastern allies, like Jordan and Egypt, with their own Palestinian populations, can feel the conflict's reverberations. Their stability is crucial to American interests, and unrest stemming from the Palestinian-Israeli issue can threaten this equilibrium.

An anecdote worth noting: In 1990, a U.S. diplomat in Jordan was taken aback when a Jordanian official, during a discussion on water security, interjected with a passionate plea about the Palestinian plight. The message was clear: even in unrelated dialogues, the conflict's specter looms large.

Economic Repercussions: The Middle East is a vital hub for global trade and energy. Prolonged instability can disrupt global markets, impacting American businesses and consumers.

Global Peace Efforts: The conflict often becomes a litmus test in international relations, straining ties between nations and impacting global cohesion. Moreover, as other countries invest diplomatic capital in this issue, it detracts from a united front on other global challenges.

American Troops and Assets: Given its commitment to Israel's security and its assets in the region, any escalation might necessitate a more direct U.S. military involvement, placing American assets and personnel at risk.

Moral Implications: The U.S. prides itself on upholding human rights and democratic values. The suffering in the Palestinian territories poses a moral question, impacting America's image on the world stage.

In wrapping up, the Palestinian-Israeli conflict's ramifications stretch far beyond its immediate locale. For the U.S., the stakes are multifaceted, intertwining national security, global peace efforts, and the nation's moral standing. Addressing this issue isn't just a matter of regional stability, but a cornerstone in the quest for a more peaceful world.

Conclusion

The Road Ahead: Prospects for Peace

The Palestinian-Israeli conflict, with its convoluted history and entrenched positions, may seem an insurmountable challenge. Yet, history has shown that even the fiercest conflicts can find resolutions. The question is: what might the road to peace in this region look like?

Two-State Solution: Historically, the most widely accepted solution has been the creation of two separate states for two peoples. This, however, requires mutual recognition, defined borders, and assurances for security. Many hurdles remain, such as the status of Jerusalem and the right of return for Palestinian refugees.

One-State Solution: Some argue for a single democratic state, where both Jews and Palestinians live with equal rights. Yet, this poses challenges surrounding the preservation of a Jewish-majority state and ensuring equal rights for everyone.

Regional Initiatives: As neighboring countries grow weary of the conflict, there's hope that they might play a constructive role in mediating between the parties. The Abraham Accords of 2020, where certain Arab nations normalized relations with Israel, hinted at a regional shift.

There's an old anecdote from the early 1990s, after the Oslo Accords were signed. An Israeli and a Palestinian, former foes, found themselves sharing a taxi in Tel Aviv. They began to discuss the future. Despite their differences, by the end of the ride, they'd planned a joint business venture. The story underscores a simple truth: at the heart of politics and conflict are people, and people can find common ground in the most unexpected ways.

Grassroots Movements: While official negotiations are crucial, the importance of grassroots initiatives, where regular Israelis and Palestinians work together, can't be understated. These efforts humanize the "other" and lay the groundwork for mutual understanding.

International Mediation: The involvement of international players, like the U.S., EU, and the UN, remains crucial. An unbiased mediator can offer a fresh perspective, resources, and incentives for peace.

Challenges Ahead: Trust remains the biggest challenge. Years of violence and distrust can't be wiped away overnight. Building trust requires leadership, patience, and, most importantly, a will to peace from both sides.

In conclusion, the path to peace is neither straight nor easy. However, with concerted efforts, empathy, and international cooperation, there's hope that the next chapters in the Palestinian-Israeli story might be about reconciliation and shared prosperity.

Role of International Community and Individuals

The Palestinian-Israeli issue isn't merely a regional concern; its repercussions resonate globally. The international community, comprising states, organizations, and individuals, plays an influential role in the trajectory of the conflict and potential peace efforts.

United Nations: Since its inception, the UN has been deeply involved, starting with the 1947 Partition Plan. Various UN bodies, like the UNRWA, provide aid to Palestinian refugees, while the Security Council has passed numerous resolutions, aiming to guide the path to peace.

Major World Powers: The U.S. has traditionally played the role of a mediator, especially in the Camp David Accords and the Oslo process. Other significant actors, such as Russia, China, and the EU, also influence diplomatic channels and offer economic incentives for peace initiatives.

Neighboring Arab States: Their stance has evolved from outright opposition, evident in the Khartoum Resolution's "Three No's" in 1967, to a more nuanced approach, showcased by the Arab Peace Initiative in 2002.

Non-Governmental Organizations (NGOs): Many NGOs work tirelessly in the region, offering humanitarian aid, facilitating dialogue, and documenting human rights abuses. Their on-ground perspectives often shape international perceptions.

Now, for an anecdote: In the 1990s, a unique initiative named "Seeds of Peace" began. Founded by journalist John Wallach, this summer camp in Maine, USA, invited young Israelis and Palestinians. Here, amidst the serene lakes and tall pines, erstwhile "enemies" played soccer, shared meals, and sang together. By summer's end, many realized the "other side" had faces, stories, and dreams much like their own. The success of this initiative demonstrates the impact individuals and civil society can have.

Role of Individuals: Beyond formal channels, individuals globally, whether diaspora communities, activists, or concerned citizens, shape narratives and influence policy. Grassroots movements, petitions, and even art and literature can spotlight issues and pressurize governments.

Public Opinion: International public sentiment, shaped by media, can sway government policies. During Israel's operations in Gaza, global protests showcased the international community's concerns and prompted diplomatic responses.

In conclusion, while the conflict's core is local, the web of influence is global. From the bustling halls of the UN in New York to a quiet summer camp in Maine, the quest for Palestinian-Israeli peace is a shared endeavor, reflecting the interconnected world we inhabit.

Encouraging Critical Thinking and Empathy

Understanding the Palestinian-Israeli conflict is a multifaceted challenge, often clouded by deeply rooted emotions, historical narratives, and polarized opinions. Encouraging critical thinking and empathy is essential for informed, balanced perspectives and constructive dialogues.

Dissecting the Narrative: Often, the narratives are binary: one side's gain is the other's loss. But history is rarely black and white. Critical thinking requires recognizing the gray areas, where both parties have legitimate grievances and rights. Analyzing the sources of information and questioning prevalent narratives can help untangle biases and offer a more holistic view.

Empathy in Action: Empathy doesn't mean sidelining one's beliefs or convictions. It entails understanding and acknowledging the feelings, hardships, and aspirations of both Palestinians and Israelis.

Here's an anecdote that captures the essence of empathy. In the early 2000s, a Palestinian father named Bassam Aramin and an Israeli father named Rami Elhanan both lost their daughters due to the conflict. Instead of succumbing to hatred, both fathers joined the "Parents Circle-Families Forum", a joint Palestinian-Israeli organization of families who have lost a member to the ongoing conflict. Through shared grief, they understood each other's pain and became advocates for peace, showing that empathy can bridge even the deepest divides.

Educational Initiatives: Promoting peace education in schools and communities can sow seeds of understanding. Programs that facilitate interactions between Israeli and Palestinian youths, like the aforementioned "Seeds of Peace", can be instrumental.

Media's Role: Media outlets have a responsibility to present unbiased facts, highlighting human stories from both sides. When media becomes a platform for shared narratives, it fosters empathy.

Digital Era & Global Connectivity: Social media platforms provide an avenue for Israelis and Palestinians to share their everyday experiences, breaking stereotypes and humanizing the "other". Platforms like Twitter and Facebook have seen numerous initiatives where common people from both sides engage in heart-to-heart conversations.

In wrapping up, the essence of approaching the Palestinian-Israeli issue with critical thinking and empathy is beautifully encapsulated in a quote by historian Howard Zinn: "To be hopeful in bad times is not just foolishly romantic. It is based on the fact that human history is a history not only of cruelty but also of compassion, sacrifice, courage, kindness."

By fostering these virtues, society takes a step closer to understanding, dialogue, and ultimately, peace.

Appendix

Key Historical Documents and Treaties

1. Balfour Declaration
  - ✓ Date: November 2, 1917
  - ✓ Proposed by: British Foreign Secretary, Arthur Balfour
  - ✓ Participants: Primarily the British government, intended for Lord Rothschild, a leader of the British Jewish community.
  - ✓ Outcome: A letter promising British support for the establishment of a "national home for the Jewish people" in Palestine, without prejudice to the rights of existing non-Jewish communities.
  - ✓ Success: While this paved the way for Jewish immigration to Palestine, it also sowed seeds for Arab resentment due to perceived betrayal by the British.

2. UN Partition Plan (Resolution 181)
  - ✓ Date: November 29, 1947
  - ✓ Proposed by: United Nations Special Committee on Palestine
  - ✓ Participants: Members of the United Nations General Assembly
  - ✓ Outcome: A recommendation to partition Palestine into Jewish and Arab states, with Jerusalem under international administration.
  - ✓ Success: Unsuccessful in its entirety. While Israel declared independence based on this partition, the Arab states rejected it, leading to the 1948 Arab-Israeli War.

3. Camp David Accords
  - ✓ Date: September 17, 1978
  - ✓ Proposed by: US President Jimmy Carter
  - ✓ Participants: Egyptian President Anwar Sadat and Israeli Prime Minister Menachem Begin.
  - ✓ Outcome: Framework for peace in the Middle East and a peace treaty between Egypt and Israel.
  - ✓ Success: Successful in leading to the Israel-Egypt Peace Treaty (March 1979), which has held since.

4. Oslo Accords
  - ✓ Date: 1993 (Oslo I) and 1995 (Oslo II)
  - ✓ Proposed by: Secret negotiations facilitated by Norway.
  - ✓ Participants: Israel and the Palestine Liberation Organization

(PLO).
- ✓ Outcome: A phased approach to Palestinian self-rule, with the establishment of the Palestinian Authority and a plan for comprehensive peace talks.
- ✓ Success: Mixed. While it led to mutual recognition and the establishment of Palestinian self-rule in parts of the West Bank and Gaza, many issues remained unresolved and trust deteriorated over the years.

5. Roadmap for Peace
- ✓ Date: April 30, 2003
- ✓ Proposed by: The Quartet (US, UN, EU, and Russia)
- ✓ Participants: Israel and Palestinians.
- ✓ Outcome: A plan proposing a two-state solution with clear phases, timelines, and reciprocal confidence-building measures.
- ✓ Success: Unsuccessful, as both sides accused the other of non-compliance and violence escalated in the subsequent years.

6. Arab Peace Initiative
- ✓ Date: March 28, 2002
- ✓ Proposed by: Then Crown Prince Abdullah of Saudi Arabia, endorsed by the Arab League.
- ✓ Participants: 22 Arab states.
- ✓ Outcome: A collective offer by Arab states to recognize Israel and establish normal relations in exchange for Israel's full withdrawal from occupied territories and a "just solution" to the Palestinian refugee issue.
- ✓ Success: Israel responded cautiously and no substantial progress was made based on the initiative.

This list provides a snapshot of the most prominent documents and treaties. Several other resolutions, negotiations, and summits have taken place over the decades with varying degrees of success.

Glossary of Terms

- **Al-Aqsa Mosque**: The third holiest site in Islam, located on the Temple Mount in Jerusalem.
- **Arab League**: A regional organization of Arab countries in and around North Africa and the Middle East.
- **Balfour Declaration**: A 1917 British statement supporting the establishment of a Jewish homeland in Palestine.
- **Diaspora**: Scattering of a population from its original homeland. Often refers to Jewish communities living outside Israel.
- **Fatah**: A Palestinian nationalist political party and the largest faction of the PLO.
- **Gaza Strip**: A narrow territory along the Mediterranean, bordered by Israel and Egypt, primarily inhabited by Palestinians.
- **Hamas**: An Islamist Palestinian organization, with a political and a militant wing, currently governing the Gaza Strip.
- **Intifada**: A Palestinian uprising against Israeli rule. There have been two major intifadas, the first beginning in 1987 and the second in 2000.
- **Iron Dome**: An air defense system developed by Israel to intercept short-range rockets and artillery shells.
- **Judaism**: The monotheistic Abrahamic religion of the Jews.
- **Knesset**: The unicameral national legislature of Israel.
- **Likud**: A right-wing political party in Israel.
- **Mandate**: A legal status for certain territories transferred from the control of one country to another, as was the case with the British Mandate for Palestine.
- **Mossad**: The national intelligence agency of Israel, responsible for intelligence gathering, covert operations, and counterterrorism.
- **Nakba**: Arabic for "catastrophe." Refers to the displacement of Palestinian Arabs following the establishment of Israel in 1948.
- **Netanyahu, Benjamin**: A prominent Israeli politician and the longest-serving Prime Minister of Israel.
- **Oslo Accords**: A set of agreements between Israel and the PLO in the

1990s, which marked a start to the peace process.

- **Palestine Liberation Organization (PLO):** An organization founded to achieve the establishment of an independent Palestinian state.
- **Palestinian Authority (PA):** The interim self-government body established in 1994 to govern parts of the West Bank and Gaza Strip.
- **Rabin, Yitzhak:** Former Israeli Prime Minister and key figure in the Oslo Accords, assassinated in 1995.
- **Right of Return:** The belief that Palestinian refugees, and their descendants, have a right to return to the homes they fled or were expelled from in 1948.
- **Settlements:** Jewish Israeli communities built on lands occupied by Israel since the 1967 Six-Day War.
- **Sharon, Ariel:** Former Israeli Prime Minister known for his controversial policies and the unilateral disengagement plan.
- **Six-Day War:** A 1967 conflict in which Israel captured the Sinai Peninsula, Gaza Strip, West Bank, East Jerusalem, and the Golan Heights.
- **Temple Mount:** A hill in Jerusalem that's sacred to both Jews and Muslims. Site of the First and Second Temples in Judaism.
- **Two-State Solution:** A proposed solution to the conflict envisioning two states for two groups of people: Israel for the Jewish people and Palestine for the Palestinian people.
- **UNRWA:** United Nations Relief and Works Agency for Palestine Refugees.
- **West Bank:** An area located west of the Jordan River, occupied by Israel during the Six-Day War and home to many Palestinian communities.
- **Yom Kippur War:** A war fought by a coalition of Arab states led by Egypt and Syria against Israel in 1973.
- **Zion:** A hill in Jerusalem, and the symbolic heart of the city. Often used as a metonym for Jerusalem and the biblical land of Israel.
- **Zionism:** A nationalist and political movement of Jews and Jewish culture that supports the re-establishment of a Jewish homeland in the territory defined as the historic Land of Israel.

Recommended Further Reading and Resources

Books:

1. **"A Peace to End All Peace" by David Fromkin**: A detailed account of the Middle Eastern political landscape after World War I.
2. **"The Question of Palestine" by Edward Said**: An introspective into the Palestinian perspective of the Israeli-Palestinian conflict.
3. **"My Promised Land: The Triumph and Tragedy of Israel" by Ari Shavit**: Chronicles Israel's history while reflecting on its future.
4. **"Palestine: Peace Not Apartheid" by Jimmy Carter**: The former U.S. President's views on the Israeli-Palestinian conflict.
5. **"The Israel-Arab Reader: A Documentary History of the Middle East Conflict" by Walter Laqueur** and Barry Rubin: A compilation of essential readings concerning the conflict.
6. **"The Iron Wall: Israel and the Arab World" by Avi Shlaim**: An exploration of Israeli foreign policy and the relationship with its neighbors.
7. **"Jerusalem: The Biography" by Simon Sebag Montefiore**: A detailed history of the city of Jerusalem.
8. **"Six Days of War: June 1967 and the Making of the Modern Middle East" by Michael B. Oren**: A detailed account of the Six-Day War.
9. **"The Ethnic Cleansing of Palestine" by Ilan Pappé**: A controversial perspective on the events of 1948.
10. **"The Lemon Tree: An Arab, a Jew, and the Heart of the Middle East" by Sandy Tolan**: A personal narrative using a single house and its various inhabitants to tell a larger story of the region.

Films:

1. **"Paradise Now" (2005)**: A film that delves into the lives of two Palestinian men preparing for a suicide attack in Israel.
2. **"Waltz with Bashir" (2008)**: An animated documentary that recounts an Israeli film director's attempt to recover blacked-out memories of his experience during the 1982 Lebanon War.

3. **"The Gatekeepers" (2012):** Interviews with six former leaders of the Israeli security agency, Shin Bet, about their perspectives and actions.
4. **"5 Broken Cameras" (2011):** A Palestinian farmer's chronicle of his nonviolent resistance to the actions of the Israeli army.
5. **"Miral" (2010):** Depicts the journey of a Palestinian girl growing up in the wake of the Arab-Israeli war.

Online Resources:

1. **B'Tselem**: An Israeli human rights organization that provides reports on the Israeli-Palestinian conflict.
https://www.btselem.org/

2. **Palestinian Centre for Human Rights (PCHR):** Provides extensive documentation on human rights violations in the Palestinian territories.
https://pchrgaza.org/en/

3. **Jewish Virtual Library:** Comprehensive information on Jewish history, Israel, U.S.-Israel relations, and the Holocaust.
https://www.jewishvirtuallibrary.org/

4. **Institute for Palestine Studies:** A leading research institute on Palestinian affairs and the Arab-Israeli conflict.
https://www.palestine-studies.org/

5. **Al Monitor:** A media site that provides reporting and analysis from and about the Middle East. https://www.al-monitor.com/

These recommendations can serve as a starting point for those keen to deepen their understanding of the complex history, narratives, and dynamics of the Israeli-Palestinian conflict.

Bonus Part: Intelligence Services - Shadows of the Israeli-Palestinian Dynamics

Introduction:

In the labyrinthine corridors of Middle Eastern politics, intelligence services often play a role as mysterious as it is influential. Their stealthy operations, sometimes recounted in hushed stories, have helped shape not just the Israeli-Palestinian dynamics but also the wider geopolitics of the region.

Consider a tale often whispered among intelligence circles. In the early 1960s, a high-ranking official received an anonymous message at his office in Jerusalem. The note contained detailed plans of an assassination attempt on an Israeli figure. No agency, no name—just a warning. To this day, debates rage about the sender's identity: was it a Palestinian informant, a double agent, or an external player? While the anecdote's full veracity remains cloaked in the annals of espionage, it underscores a key theme: the nebulous line between friend and foe in the world of shadows.

For Israel and Palestine, their intelligence apparatus isn't just about espionage. It's an intricate dance of defense and offense, of securing national interests while navigating the treacherous waters of international relations. From Mossad's operations that reach far beyond Israel's borders to the fragmented yet formidable Palestinian intelligence factions, these entities have played pivotal roles in wars, peace negotiations, and everything in between.

As we delve into this bonus chapter, we'll lift the curtain, albeit slightly, on these intelligence behemoths. We'll trace their histories, their operations, their successes, and their controversies. And as we tread, we'll come to recognize the weight of their influence not just on the Israeli-Palestinian saga but on the very fabric of global geopolitics.

The world of intelligence—where every piece of information can be a game-changer, and every shadow might just be telling a story. Let's begin this intriguing journey.

Chapter 15: Israel's Mossad - Beyond Espionage

Historical Evolution: Tracing the roots of Mossad, its establishment, and early operations.

In the post-war world of the 1940s, as nations reeled and rebuilt, Israel found itself in a unique position. Born amidst regional antagonism, the fledgling nation's need for a robust intelligence service was paramount. Enter Mossad—Israel's answer to this imperative, its eye and ear in a complex world.

The roots of Mossad can be traced back to the very creation of Israel in 1948. However, its formal establishment came in December 1951, under the leadership of then Prime Minister David Ben-Gurion. Its title, "Mossad," simply means "institute," but its mandate was anything but simple: intelligence collection, covert operations, and counterterrorism.

In its early years, Mossad was pivotal in operations like Operation Magic Carpet, which airlifted thousands of Yemenite Jews to Israel in 1949. Such missions highlighted Mossad's dual role in both espionage and ensuring the welfare of Jewish communities globally.

A tale that captures Mossad's audacity in its early days revolves around the abduction of Adolf Eichmann, a principal architect of the Holocaust. In a daring 1960 operation, Mossad agents captured Eichmann from

Argentina and smuggled him to Israel. Ensuing was a globally-publicized trial, ensuring the world would not forget the horrors of the Holocaust. This operation wasn't just an act of justice but a stark message of Israel's global reach and its commitment to the Jewish diaspora.

However, Mossad's journey wasn't without missteps. Early operations saw failures, and the agency underwent several overhauls to refine its methods and structures.

As Mossad matured, its operations grew in scale and sophistication, making it one of the most respected—and feared—intelligence agencies in the world. Yet, at its core, Mossad's mission remained consistent: to ensure the safety and security of Israel and Jews worldwide. From navigating the intricacies of Cold War politics to confronting emerging threats, the Mossad has been at the forefront, shaping, and sometimes shaking, the geopolitical stage.

Operational Reach: An overview of Mossad's wide-ranging operations - from espionage and counterterrorism to protection of Jewish communities worldwide.

With its inception rooted in the tumultuous Middle East, Mossad swiftly recognized that its operational arena would not be limited to its immediate neighbors. As Israel's external intelligence agency, its operational reach would span continents, reflecting the global nature of threats and challenges Israel faced.

1. **Espionage**: One cannot discuss Mossad without acknowledging its reputation for international espionage. The agency's operatives have been embedded in countless countries, gathering vital

intelligence. This intelligence ranged from technological advancements of adversaries to insights into regional alliances and enmities. Mossad's success here can be attributed to its ability to blend human intelligence ("HUMINT") with technological tools, often putting it steps ahead of its opponents.

2. **Counterterrorism**: Beyond traditional espionage, Mossad has been at the forefront of Israel's counterterrorism efforts. After the tragic 1972 Munich Olympics, where 11 Israeli athletes were murdered by the Palestinian group Black September, Mossad launched Operation Wrath of God. This covert operation targeted those involved in the Munich massacre, showcasing Mossad's determination to reach adversaries beyond borders. An anecdote that epitomizes their relentless pursuit is the case of Ali Hassan Salameh, the alleged mastermind behind the Munich attack. After several failed attempts, Mossad agents finally located and assassinated him in Beirut in 1979. Such operations have painted Mossad as an agency that never forgets nor forgives.

3. **Protection of Jewish Communities**: While espionage and counterterrorism often grab headlines, Mossad's mandate extends to the protection of Jewish communities globally. In regions where Jews faced persecution or existential threats, Mossad orchestrated their safe evacuation. Operations like Solomon and Joshua in the 1980s and 90s facilitated the airlift of Ethiopian Jews facing dire conditions. Similarly, Operation Yachin in the 1960s safely transported Moroccan Jews to Israel. These operations underscore Mossad's commitment to the idea of Israel as a sanctuary for Jews worldwide.

As the world evolves, so too does Mossad's operational palette. Cyber warfare, disinformation campaigns, and the increasing relevance of non-state actors have ensured that Mossad remains adaptive, innovative, and ever-watchful. However, its core mission remains unchanged: the protection of the State of Israel and Jewish communities, no matter where they might be.

Key Operations & Controversies: Highlighting some of the most notable (and publicly known) operations and the ethical debates surrounding them.

The covert nature of intelligence work invariably leads to operations that spark both admiration and controversy. Mossad, with its global reach and high-profile targets, has had its fair share of both. Some operations are lauded for their precision and audacity, while others raise moral and ethical concerns.

1. **Operation Entebbe (1976):** In a dramatic rescue mission that sounds straight out of a thriller novel, Mossad played a pivotal role in rescuing 102 hostages from Entebbe Airport in Uganda. After an Air France plane was hijacked by two Palestinian and two German terrorists, the hostages, mainly Israelis, were kept at the old terminal of the airport. Mossad agents quickly gathered intelligence on the ground situation, enabling the Israel Defense Forces to execute a daring raid that resulted in the rescue of all but four of the hostages. The mission's success was a significant morale boost, showcasing Mossad's and IDF's capabilities.
   Anecdote: One of the key elements that ensured the mission's success was a replica of the airport terminal in Uganda, built in Israel based on the intelligence

provided. This allowed the commandos to practice and refine their approach, ensuring minimal casualties during the actual raid.

2. **Assassination of Gerald Bull (1990):** Gerald Bull, a Canadian ballistic engineer, was assisting Iraq in building a supergun that had the potential to alter the balance of power in the region. While Mossad neither confirmed nor denied involvement, it's widely believed that they orchestrated Bull's assassination in Brussels. The ethical debate here revolves around the legitimacy of extrajudicial killings, even when national security is potentially at stake.

3. **Mabhouh Assassination (2010):** Mahmoud al-Mabhouh, a senior Hamas military commander, was assassinated in his hotel room in Dubai. While Mossad never claimed responsibility, the intricate operation involving multiple agents and disguises was attributed to them. The use of European passports by the operatives raised diplomatic tensions with the concerned countries. The operation stirred debates about the ethical implications of assassinations on foreign soil and the potential abuse of allied nations' trust.

4. **Operation Orchard (2007):** In a stealth operation, Israeli jets destroyed a facility in Syria, which Israel, the US, and IAEA believed was a nuclear reactor being built with North Korean assistance. Mossad's intelligence was pivotal in identifying and locating the facility. The controversy here was multi-fold - from the violation of another country's sovereignty to the potential escalation of hostilities in the region.

5. **Prisoner X (2010):** The mysterious case of "Prisoner X," later identified as Ben Zygier, an Australian-Israeli citizen and alleged Mossad agent, who died in an Israeli prison, raised questions about Mossad's internal workings, the treatment of its agents, and the

lengths to which information is kept secret even from allies.

The work of intelligence agencies, Mossad included, is often shrouded in secrecy, necessitating difficult choices in gray areas of morality and ethics. While many of Mossad's operations have been heralded for their efficacy and precision, they have not been without criticisms and controversies, underscoring the complex nature of intelligence work in the modern era.

Chapter 16: Palestinian Intelligence - Fragmented Yet Formidable

Emergence and Evolution: The Creation and Development of Various Palestinian Intelligence Arms Amidst a Fragmented Political Landscape

The complex tapestry of the Middle East, with its myriad factions, ideologies, and allegiances, provides a backdrop for the evolution of Palestinian intelligence. Over the decades, Palestinian entities, largely in response to a shifting political landscape, have fostered their intelligence capabilities, evolving them as necessary.

1. **Pre-Oslo Era**: Before the establishment of the Palestinian Authority (PA) in 1994, Palestinian intelligence operations were mainly orchestrated by various factions within the Palestine Liberation Organization (PLO). These factions conducted intelligence, counter-intelligence, and covert operations primarily against Israel and occasionally against each other.
Anecdote: It's often rumored that intelligence operatives during this era would use coded messages

in seemingly mundane items like grocery lists or newspaper ads to communicate covertly.

2. **The Birth of the Palestinian Authority**: With the Oslo Accords, the PA was established, and it soon began forming its official intelligence arms. The General Intelligence Service (also known as Mukhabarat) and the Preventive Security Service (PSS) emerged as the two dominant entities. While both had roles in counter-intelligence and maintaining internal security, the Mukhabarat primarily focused on external threats, and the PSS dealt with internal matters, especially those related to Hamas and Islamic Jihad.

3. **The Hamas Factor**: Hamas, in stark contrast to Fatah and the PA, developed its intelligence capabilities more clandestinely. After its 2006 election victory and subsequent takeover of the Gaza Strip in 2007, Hamas established its own formal intelligence services. Its military wing, the Izz ad-Din al-Qassam Brigades, played a pivotal role in intelligence operations, particularly against Israel.

4. **Post-Oslo Fragmentation**: The rivalry between Fatah (dominating the West Bank) and Hamas (controlling Gaza) has led to parallel intelligence structures. Each side has occasionally used its intelligence apparatus against the other, leading to instances of internal strife and further complicating peace and unity efforts.

5. **Modern-Day Challenges**: Today, Palestinian intelligence agencies grapple with numerous challenges. Balancing between counteracting Israeli intelligence operations, maintaining internal stability, and navigating the turbulent waters of intra-Palestinian politics requires agility and adaptability.

In essence, the evolution of Palestinian intelligence is a

reflection of the region's broader political developments. As the aspirations of the Palestinian people have shifted and adapted, so too have the mechanisms designed to protect and advocate for those aspirations. Through all its phases, the central theme remains constant: a people striving for recognition, statehood, and a brighter future in a challenging landscape.

Key Players: A Look at the Dominant Intelligence Bodies, Including Those Affiliated with Fatah, Hamas, and Other Factions

Navigating the intricate maze of Palestinian politics reveals a complex web of intelligence bodies, each with its unique origin, agenda, and function. These entities, while all operating under the broad umbrella of Palestinian aspirations, often possess diverging methodologies and priorities.

1. **General Intelligence Service (Mukhabarat):** A significant pillar of the Palestinian Authority's (PA) intelligence architecture, Mukhabarat primarily focuses on external threats. Operating largely in the West Bank, it has been involved in liaisons with intelligence agencies of other countries, including coordination with the CIA and counterparts in the Arab world.
   Anecdote: In a rather unusual act of camaraderie, an Israeli and a Palestinian intelligence officer, who were known to be fierce adversaries in the field, once found themselves stranded due to a sandstorm during a covert meeting in a third country. The ensuing hours, as per unofficial tales, involved shared meals, music, and stories, reflecting the deep-seated human desires that sometimes get overshadowed by political

agendas.

2. **Preventive Security Service (PSS):** Often viewed as the PA's primary internal security agency, the PSS functions mainly in the West Bank. With a focus on internal threats, it keeps a close eye on opposition groups, especially those affiliated with Hamas.

3. **Izz ad-Din al-Qassam Brigades**: The military wing of Hamas, this entity is more than just an armed faction. It conducts intelligence and counter-intelligence operations, particularly against Israel, and has been instrumental in numerous operations, including kidnappings and tunneling activities.

4. **Hamas Internal Security**: Post its takeover of Gaza in 2007, Hamas set up its formal intelligence structure, handling matters of internal security in Gaza, and has been crucial in curbing dissent and monitoring potential threats from Fatah and other rival groups.

5. **Other Factions**: Beyond the primary players of Fatah and Hamas, groups like Islamic Jihad and the Popular Front for the Liberation of Palestine (PFLP) have their own intelligence operations, albeit on a smaller scale. Their focus tends to oscillate between resistance against Israel and navigating their space within the broader Palestinian political spectrum.

As these entities play their roles on the intelligence chessboard, their moves are emblematic of the larger Palestinian narrative: a blend of resistance, aspiration, internal rivalry, and the perennial pursuit of statehood. They are a testament to the old adage that in the realm of intelligence and geopolitics, the only constant is change.

Operations and Challenges: Exploring Notable Operations, Internal Challenges, and the Difficulties Posed by Factional Rivalries

Palestinian intelligence operations are as multifaceted as the political landscape from which they emerge. They've orchestrated commendable feats, countered security threats, and sometimes been mired in the messy web of inter-factional discord. Delving into this world uncovers tales of valiant operatives, elusive spies, and the constant challenge of navigating an intricate political maze.

1. **Notable Operations:**
   - **Tunneling Endeavors**: Especially prominent in Gaza, the tunnel networks serve multiple purposes – from smuggling essential goods to launching surprise attacks against Israeli targets. Their strategic importance can't be overstated.
   - **Collaborations for Prisoner Exchanges**: Operations aimed at capturing Israeli soldiers for future exchanges have, at times, led to significant prisoner swaps, most famously the Gilad Shalit exchange in 2011.

   Anecdote: A Palestinian operative, code-named "The Mole," once managed to infiltrate a rival faction for years, feeding vital information to his handlers. His true identity was protected not just by his wits, but also by his ability to seamlessly adapt to new personas, even mastering different regional dialects to perfection.

2. **Internal Challenges:**
   - **Inter-faction Rivalries:** Often, the greatest challenges come from within. For instance, the PSS's constant endeavors to suppress Hamas

in the West Bank, or Hamas's counter-efforts against Fatah in Gaza, demonstrate the friction between the two dominant factions.

- **Information Leaks**: With many operatives and sympathizers embedded across factions, information leaks have sometimes jeopardized critical operations.

3. **Difficulties from Factional Rivalries:**
    - **Fragmented Communication**: Different factions possess different sources of intelligence, leading to a fragmented view of potential threats or opportunities. This lack of unified information sometimes compromises the broader Palestinian strategic objectives.
    - **Trust Deficit**: A history of suspicion means intelligence sharing between factions, even when it does occur, is often marred by doubts about the authenticity or completeness of the shared data.
    - **Dual Loyalties**: Some operatives, due to family ties or personal history, have loyalties to more than one faction. This can lead to conflicts of interest and challenge the primary allegiance of these individuals.

In the shadows of these operations and challenges lies the true resilience of the Palestinian intelligence entities. Their narratives, while unique in specific details, mirror a larger global intelligence truth: the realm of espionage is not just about external adversaries, but often, the internal dynamics pose the most intricate challenges.

Chapter 17: Espionage and Peace - The Double-Edged Sword

Intelligence in Peace Negotiations: The Two-Sided Coin of Assistance and Hindrance

In the complex tapestry of the Israeli-Palestinian conflict, intelligence operations weave threads both visible and hidden. These operations, while primarily focused on security and strategic advantages, have indirectly and directly impacted peace negotiations over the decades. Like two sides of a coin, they've offered insights beneficial for peace, but simultaneously, their very nature has at times bred mistrust.

1. **Intelligence as a Facilitator:**
   - **Backchannel Diplomacy:** Quiet, covert communications have historically played a role in bridging gaps. These unofficial channels, often facilitated by intelligence agencies, have paved the way for formal negotiations. By operating behind the scenes, they can explore compromise without the glare of public scrutiny.
   - **Information Sharing for Mutual Benefit:** At times, both sides have seen the value in sharing specific intelligence, particularly when it concerns mutual threats. Such moments of cooperation, though brief, build a certain level of trust.

   Anecdote: In the early 2000s, a covert meeting between Israeli and Palestinian intelligence officers took place in a nondescript European city. The rendezvous, unknown to the public and many in the government, wasn't about espionage – it was about finding common ground. Over cups of black coffee, they discussed shared concerns about extremist factions. This quiet conversation paved the way for several confidence-building measures in the months that followed.

2. **Intelligence as a Stumbling Block:**
   - Acts of Espionage and Their Fallout: Instances where covert operations have been exposed can breed mistrust. For instance, when one side uncovers spies within their ranks or operations aimed at destabilizing their leadership, it becomes challenging to sit across the negotiating table in good faith.
   - **Use of Intelligence as Leverage**: Intelligence, when used as a bargaining chip or to pressurize the other side, can backfire. Revelations or threats to reveal compromising information about the other party can halt peace talks before they even begin.
   - **Perceived Biases:** Intelligence, by its nature, operates in shades of gray. Reports, especially when leaked, can be seen as biased or partial, leading to suspicions about the true intentions of the other side.

In conclusion, while intelligence operations are primarily tactical and strategic tools, their ripples often touch the shores of diplomacy. The challenge for peace negotiators, then, is to harness the positive potentials of these operations while navigating their pitfalls with care and foresight.

Trust and Distrust: Intelligence's Dual Role in Crafting Perceptions

The Israeli-Palestinian narrative is rich in history, passion, and hope, but it is also shadowed by an underlying theme of mistrust. Central to this narrative is the role of intelligence operations. Like actors on a stage, these agencies both illuminate and cast shadows, playing pivotal roles in fostering trust or deepening divisions.

1. **Building Trust Through Intelligence:**
   - **Shared Threats:** When both sides face a common enemy or threat, intelligence sharing becomes a tool for collaboration. This collaborative stance, even if short-lived, can bridge gaps, signaling that common interests do exist.
   - **Transparent Overtones:** Occasionally, both parties have allowed certain intelligence operations to be more "visible" as a gesture of goodwill or to signify transparency.

   Anecdote: In the 1990s, a Hamas splinter group posed threats to both Israelis and the Palestinian Authority. In a rare move, discreet intelligence sharing between the two sides helped thwart an imminent attack. This cooperation, though not publicized, played a subtle role in warming relations during that period.

2. **Deepening Distrust Through Covert Operations:**
   - **Counterintelligence Failures:** When one side successfully infiltrates the other, the exposed operations can fan the flames of mistrust. The feeling of being "watched" or "betrayed" creates barriers in dialogue and diplomacy.
   - **Disinformation:** Intelligence agencies sometimes employ tactics of spreading false information. Such operations, when revealed, only reinforce the narrative that the other side is not to be trusted.
   - **Targeted Operations:** Assassinations, abductions, or other high-profile operations directly aimed at one side by the other can create significant setbacks in the peace process.

   Anecdote: In the early 2010s, a series of leaked

documents suggested that a particular Palestinian leader was willing to make major concessions. While the authenticity of these documents remains debated, their leak resulted in heightened suspicions. The idea that intelligence could be manipulating or playing with public perceptions only deepened the chasm of trust.

3. **The Perception Play:** Intelligence operations, even when not directly linked to peace negotiations, shape public and political perceptions. They play into the stories each side tells about the other - sometimes as protectors and at other times as provocateurs.

In the labyrinth of the Israeli-Palestinian conflict, intelligence operations act as both guides and gatekeepers. Their impact on trust is profound, reflecting the complexities of a relationship yearning for peace yet haunted by history. The challenge lies in discerning the shadows from the substance and understanding that behind every covert operation lies a narrative, a desire, and a hope for a better tomorrow.

Future Dynamics: Navigating the Uncharted Waters of Intelligence in a Digital Age

The world of intelligence, much like the broader geopolitical landscape, is never static. With every technological breakthrough, every shift in global power structures, and every new generation of leaders, the terrain of intelligence reshapes. The Israeli-Palestinian context, nested within this flux, offers a unique lens through which we can observe these dynamics.

1. **The Digital Frontier:**
   - **Cyber Espionage:** With the proliferation of digital tools and platforms, cyber-espionage has emerged as a major avenue for intelligence gathering. The potential for hacking governmental databases, critical infrastructures, and even personal accounts poses a new set of challenges and opportunities.
   - **Social Media & Open-Source Intelligence:** Platforms like Twitter and Facebook are goldmines for intelligence agencies. Not only can these be used to spread or counter narratives, but they also offer a vast array of data for analysis.

   Anecdote: A few years back, an ordinary tweet about a rally in a Palestinian city caught the eye of Israeli intelligence. Not because of its content, but because of its geolocation - revealing a new and previously unknown tunnel entrance.

2. **Emerging Technologies and Ethical Implications:**
   - **Surveillance Tech:** From drones equipped with facial recognition to AI algorithms that can predict movements based on data patterns, the tools at the disposal of intelligence agencies are growing exponentially.
   - **The Ethics of Tech:** With these advances, the debate around privacy, human rights, and the limits of surveillance becomes even more pressing. How do we draw the line between security and privacy?

3. **The Global Stage:**
   - **Shifting Alliances:** As global superpowers recalibrate their alliances and interests, intelligence operations will have to adapt. The information shared, the operations greenlit, and the strategies employed will reflect these larger geopolitical shifts.

- **Non-state Actors and Decentralization:**
  Traditional intelligence was often state-centric.
  However, with the rise of influential non-state
  actors, from tech giants to international NGOs, the
  field of players has expanded.
  Anecdote: In a surprising turn of events in the late
  2020s, a major tech corporation inadvertently derailed
  a covert operation. Their AI-driven systems flagged
  and halted an unusual transaction, only later to
  discover it was an undercover operation by a state
  actor.

In conclusion, the future of intelligence in the Israeli-
Palestinian context will be marked by rapid technological
advancements, evolving geopolitical currents, and an ever

Conclusion: A Dance in the Shadows - Intelligence and the Path Forward

The intricate tapestry of the Israeli-Palestinian conflict is
woven with threads of history, politics, religion, and deep-
seated emotions. At its backdrop, often unseen but always
present, the role of intelligence agencies has been both a
guardian and a ghost, influencing the course of events in
both obvious and subtle ways.

It is undeniable that intelligence operations have, at times,
thwarted imminent threats, preventing loss of innocent lives.
On a dark night in the 1990s, for instance, an Israeli mother
received an unexpected call. The voice on the other end
simply informed her that her son, on his way to a cafe,
should perhaps choose a different destination tonight. No
reason given, no details offered. The next day, news broke of
an averted attack at that very cafe. Incidents like these
underline the protective mantle intelligence can offer.

Yet, these agencies have also been players in deepening mistrust and animosity. Covert operations, misinformation campaigns, and the unsettling feeling of always being watched have left scars on the collective psyches of both Palestinians and Israelis.

As we look forward, intelligence, with its power to operate in the shadows, holds a dual potential. It can be a tool to foster understanding, revealing realities that push both sides towards reconciliation. Or it can further entrench divisions, adding more walls in an already divided land.

The hope is that as the world evolves, and as the Israeli-Palestinian dynamics shift, intelligence will emerge not just as a force guarding geopolitical interests, but as an architect of peace, building bridges of trust in a region yearning for it.

Thank you for your attention.

To a brighter future

The author.

Printed in Great Britain
by Amazon

29985383R00064